# The Semi-Complete Guide to Sort of Being a Gentleman

# The Semi-Complete Guide to Sort of Being a Gentleman

*Sir Gentleman Brock LaBorde, Esquire*

*Studio 8 Entertainment, LLC*
*www.studio8.net*

iUniverse, Inc.
New York  Lincoln  Shanghai

# The Semi-Complete Guide to Sort of Being a Gentleman

Copyright © 2005 by Brock LaBorde

iUniverse books may be ordered through booksellers or by contacting:

iUniverse
2021 Pine Lake Road, Suite 100
Lincoln, NE 68512
www.iuniverse.com
1-800-Authors (1-800-288-4677)

Illustrations by Truston Aillet

ISBN: 0-595-34152-7

Printed in the United States of America

*For Gentleman Brock, who wrote this book*

# Contents

An Introduction to a Gentleman . . . . . . . . . . . . . . . . . . . . . . . . . . . . . .ix

CHAPTER 1    A Gentleman in General. . . . . . . . . . . . . . . . . . . . . . .1

CHAPTER 2    The Immaculate Gentleman Who Is Able to Dress
Himself . . . . . . . . . . . . . . . . . . . . . . . . . . . . . . . . . . . 20

CHAPTER 3    A Gentleman's Dining Habits. . . . . . . . . . . . . . . . . . 32

CHAPTER 4    The Social Gentleman. . . . . . . . . . . . . . . . . . . . . . . 45

CHAPTER 5    A Gentleman Abroad . . . . . . . . . . . . . . . . . . . . . . . 60

CHAPTER 6    The Partying Gentleman. . . . . . . . . . . . . . . . . . . . . 73

CHAPTER 7    A Gentleman's Buddies. . . . . . . . . . . . . . . . . . . . . . 95

CHAPTER 8    A Gentleman on the job . . . . . . . . . . . . . . . . . . . . 106

CHAPTER 9    A Gentleman's Equipment . . . . . . . . . . . . . . . . . . 117

CHAPTER 10   Hopelessly Difficult Etiquette: A Gentleman Takes
on the Impossible. . . . . . . . . . . . . . . . . . . . . . . . . . 124

# An Introduction to a Gentleman

For centuries, perhaps decades, men have been burdened with the seemingly impossible task of remaining respectable and orderly at all times, even though they should be allowed to act however they please. But behaving keeps the women happy, and it is women who have customarily defined the standards of behavior for men to live up to. However, male etiquette experts such as Stanley Shuppinski, Cedric von Samiss, and I, Sir Gentleman Brock, Esquire, have also greatly defined and upheld these standards, all of which are enclosed in this book.

So, tender male readers, you may rest assured that by purchasing or stealing this book, you have taken the first feeble step towards becoming a gentleman. Though women have no business reading or skimming through this book, they should rejoice that it is in print, for it helps create men who are worthy and capable of engaging them in pleasant social and sexual relationships. Children, regardless of gender type, may read this book, but they should only look at the pictures.

For those foolish few male readers who remain skeptical about whether or not this book is for them, allow me to sway their pathetic, misguided opinions.

At some point in every man's life, he must leave the most influential woman in his life, his mother, unless, like myself, he can't bear the thought of living away from her endlessly intrusive, yet gentle guidance. Once on his own, every man must learn how to interact with people and find some kind of money-earning tasks to perform. He understands that he will have to deal with hundreds of grocery store clerks and thousands of carnival game operators on a daily basis.

Social situations such as these can bring about indigestion and nervous disorders for most ordinary men. One might break into tears while struggling to lace up his shoes with spaghetti noodles or while cutting the crust off a moldy sardine sandwich. One might become a stuttering fool every time he attempts to kiss the armpit of a young lady.

This is why every man must resolve to transform himself into a gentleman. A true gentleman inexplicably believes that he can make the world a better place by converting himself into the nicest, most sensitive human being possible. A gentleman understands that his entire existence is called into question every time he reaches out to take a sip from his wine glass without making sure his cufflinks stay perfectly angled so as not to cast a glare into his tablemate's eyes.

With a little ingenuity, quite a bit of natural handsomeness, and a considerable amount of one's income spent on tuxedo rentals, any dedicated individual may earn the title of "gentleman." He must also memorize literally millions of fancy rules and strict regulations.

This book is a survival guide for those would-be gentlemen who feel that they are drowning in a sea of outdated traditions and confusing rituals. Within the pages of this book, one can easily read, comprehend, and commit to memory every fancy rule and strict regulation involved with becoming a gentleman.

The world needs gentlemen and gentlemen need at least some parts of the world. Without both of these things, neither would exist. The only way a man can truly learn to be a gentleman is by being a gentleman while he is still alive. A dead gentleman does no good for anyone, though he will undoubtedly look cleaner and more respectable than someone who was not a gentleman during his lifetime.

One final warning for those brave, wise souls who wish to continue: Any man who violates *even one* of the following rules at any point in his life is *never again* worthy of being called a gentleman.

# 1

# A Gentleman in General

A gentleman allows himself to be walked on and screwed over repeatedly without once complaining about it.

A gentleman never refers to himself as a "genital-man."

A gentleman is endlessly nice and never gets laid.

A gentleman only engages in tomfoolery while in the midst of horse-playing or within 15 minutes of his last dilly-dallying.

Holding a door open for an elderly person does not make a man a gentleman. However, that and $50 in cash can make him an "Honorary Gentleman" if he knows the right people.

A gentleman never playfully aims his Salad Shooter at anyone, especially a salad.

If an item is marked "Not intended for individual resale," a gentleman does not question this.

A gentleman thinks for a minimum of fifteen minutes before every sentence he utters.

Unless he is an English teacher, a gentleman does not assign homework to others. He may assign it to himself as long as he gets someone else to grade it.

A gentleman sends a nice card and flowers to himself every time he masturbates.

A gentleman applauds loudly at the end of television programs that he is fond of. At plays and concerts, he is encouraged to mimic applause by convincingly moving his hands as if he were really clapping. Funerals require no applause or celebratory shouting, unless it is a fellow gentleman's funeral.

A gentleman always offers to share an umbrella with someone who already has one.

A gentleman always remembers to thank the chair that allowed him to occupy it, usually in the form of a thank-you letter.

A gentleman's television watching ends promptly at ten o'clock. This should pose no problem for a true gentleman, who should have been in bed by 8:30 anyway.

# The Cigar Aficionado Gentleman

A gentleman smokes a cigar in the same manner that he would drink a glass of water—whenever he is thirsty and whenever he feels the urge to do so. However, since he knows that cigar smoke is not enjoyed by everyone, the gentleman lights a few cigarettes and places them around himself to cover up the sometimes unpleasant cigar odors.

After smoking, he lights a few matches, the smell of burning sulfur helping to disguise the smell of burning tobacco. He masks the sulfur stench by spraying air freshener, then hides the air freshener with cologne, covers the cologne with perfume, and then conceals the perfume smell with Febreeze.

All floating ashes, clouds of smoke, and aerosol fogs generated during his smoke break should be sucked up into a hand-held vacuum cleaner.

# Gentlemen: Good Sports about Being Bad at Sports

If a gentleman is defeated in any type of game, he immediately pouts, accuses his victorious competitor of cheating, and vows never to play the game again. This is repeated until there are no more games in the world left for him to play. Then and only then does the gentleman accept the ungentlemanly title of a "sore loser".

A gentleman understands that playing football is for sissies, but playing pinochle is for gentlemen *and* sissies.

At the grocery checkout conveyor belt, a gentleman may make use of the plastic grocery divider stick, but only to scratch those hard-to-reach places.

If a gentleman eats in bed, he sleeps on the dining room table.

Before he attends a live sporting event, a gentleman is sure to memorize all rally chants and traditional hand gestures associated with both competing teams. This is because he understands that it is the fans' responsibility to support the players. He also knows that it is his duty to support the fans by composing a few rousing cheers of his own, which are to be performed whenever the crowd is not cheering for either of the on-field teams.

If a gentleman *despises someone*, he secretly mutilates himself out of guilt. Consequently, if a gentleman is *despised by someone*, he secretly mutilates himself out of courtesy.

A gentleman knows that a dictionary is a place of holy worship, a thesaurus is some type of frightening bird-like dinosaur, and an encyclopedia is some tiny, undeveloped country in Africa. None of these three things should be in his possession.

There is not a good movie that a gentleman has not seen or a classic book that he has not read. He simply chooses not to discuss the themes, plots, or characters of an overwhelming majority of them.

A gentleman never enters any restroom marked with a sign that reads "MEN." If he feels the urge to cleanse his digestive tract, but can find no bathroom marked "GENTLEMEN," he opts to make use of the nearest "LADIES" restroom, since ladies are essentially female versions of gentlemen.

Despite what business he is taking care of in the restroom, a gentleman always sits down on the toilet seat to avoid accidentally leaving the toilet seat in the upright position when he is finished. He also sits when using a urinal to help reinforce this good habit.

At any given time, a gentleman can cook up a mayonnaise sandwich or cup of water.

A gentleman never asks the following questions:

- "Since you two are standing next to each other, does that mean you have oral sex with one another?"

- "Why do I think of something gross when I hear your name?"

- "You don't remember my face or what I did to you a while back, do you?"

- "Can I see what size pants you are wearing?"

- "May I lick that bit of sauce off your chin?"

A gentleman attributes every quote he uses to either William Shakespeare or himself.

If a gentleman speaks French, he attempts to out-French any Frenchmen he meets.

A gentleman never tells funny jokes. What tickles one man, offends another. However, everybody loves a good tickling, and the gentleman considers this to be one of his most serious and imperative tasks in life.

When questioned, a gentleman always provides direct answers; unless he is being questioned by the police because then they would surely discover his most terrible secrets and punish him accordingly.

A gentleman does not laugh at racist, sexist, or anti-gay jokes unless they are being told by a minority, a woman, or a homosexual, because then it is okay to laugh and will probably make the poor people feel better about their pathetic shortcomings.

When a gentleman is done with the dryer, he wipes up and, without the dryer knowing, he then seduces the toaster.

A gentleman waves at blind people and shouts a friendly "Hullo!" to the deaf.

On a rainy day, a gentleman strives to cover every mud puddle he finds with an article of his clothing so that no one gets their shoes dirty.

A gentleman never says offensive words in the presence of people who are deaf, blind, retarded, or in a coma. He may, however, say whatever he wishes around those who are deaf, blind, retarded, *and* in coma.

Laundromats are wonderful places in which to pass all of a gentleman's free time. To have fun while being helpful, a gentleman may periodically smell inside each of the washers and dryers, informing everyone as to when their clothes "smell like they are ready."

# A Gentleman Stuck in a Doorway

A gentleman tediously inspects every door before he walks through it in case it might collapse on him. He should also open and close the door a few times to help keep the hinges well lubricated.

Revolving doors are not worth a gentleman's time to figure out unless he is currently employed as a professional doorman. In that case, he must make sure that the door never stops rotating as long as he is on duty.

Never should a gentleman share an elevator with another person. That type of crude behavior is reserved for children or those living in undeveloped countries. Besides, every gentleman knows that homeless folk usually set up their disease-infested temporary residences in elevators.

Immediately following a violent domestic dispute, a gentleman makes sure to ask his battered wife/boyfriend/child, "Hey, are you okay?"

A gentleman slowly sips his coffee until he is finished, even when he realizes that someone (likely not a gentleman) has replaced his coffee with rancid stomach bile as a practical joke.

A gentleman always closes the eyes of the victim he is about to bury, showing respect where it is due.

A woman may be a gentleman, too, as long as she first surgically attaches a set of fully functioning male genitalia to herself.

It is a gentleman's right and duty to immediately consent to death if someone politely asks him to die.

A gentleman drinks directly from a milk jug only if it is of 2% or higher milk fat content *and* only if it has been freshly pulled from a respectable grocery store's dumpster.

A gentleman should never assume that others will provide him with any condoms; therefore, he does not worry about that sort of thing.

A gentleman respects the 'No Shirt, No Shoes—No Service' policy of any fast food restaurant. Thus, he politely removes every piece of clothing except for his shirt and shoes *before* entering.

# How to Tie (and Use) a Noose

Tying a noose is no different than playing the piano or painting a highly cherished piece of art—it is something that cannot be learned but must be taught anyway. Gentlemen should understand this and patiently practice at home *before* they become suicidal or get caught committing a white collar crime. Part of being prepared is taking care of one's duties before they necessarily need to be done.

1. Adjust the rope's length. (A short rope is uncomfortable and awkward to work with. If the rope is too long, you will hit the ground and end up with a healthier, less dead look.)

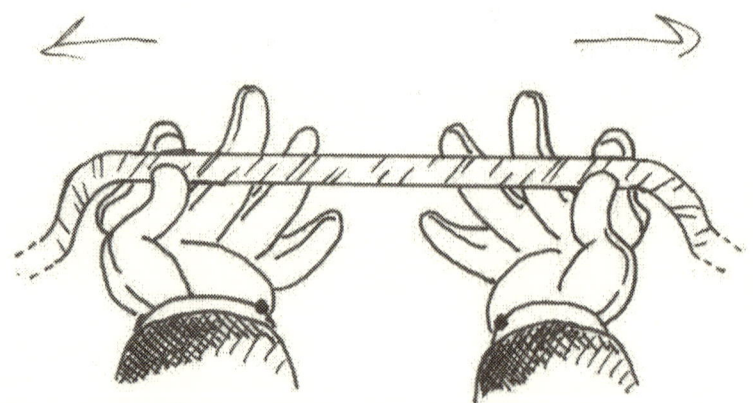

2. Loop one end of the rope around your neck. The other end needs to be anchored to a high beam or ceiling fan.

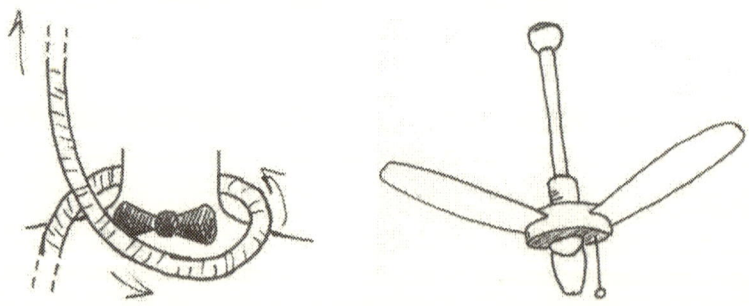

3.  Tie a good noose knot. For best results, use a "gentleman's knot," which can be effortlessly mastered by reading the book *Tying a Gentleman's Knot in 182 Easy Steps* by Sir Gentleman Brock LaBorde, Esquire.

4.  Tug on the rope to test its ability to support the weight of your swinging corpse. If necessary, install a sturdier ceiling fan or lower the ceiling beam if it is too high.

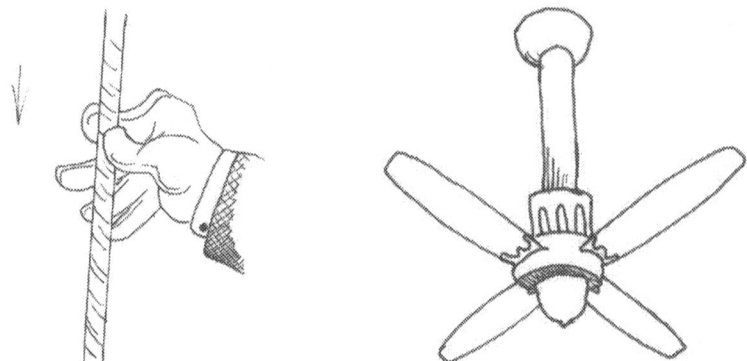

5.  Steps 1–4 need to be done while standing on a chair or on the back of a trusted friend. If you have not been doing that, start this entire pro-

cedure over. Also, if you do not want your dead body to kick the person who finds you in their head, turn off the ceiling fan.

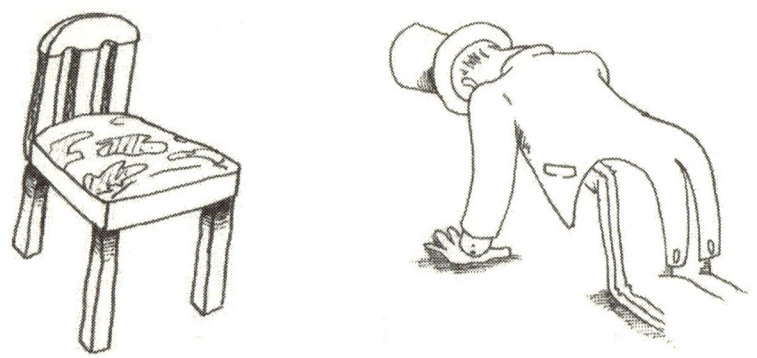

6.  Using one hand, secure the open loop around your neck. With the other hand, tighten the knot until you feel a slight hindrance to your breathing ability.

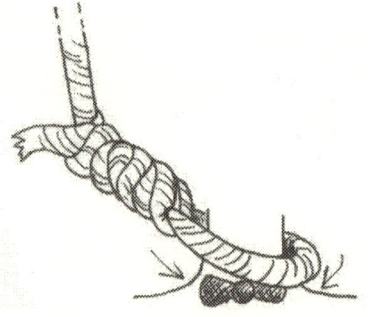

7.  Go to a different room in your house and compose a lengthy and heartfelt letter to your friends, loved ones, and houseplants, explaining why you were following the directions in this book. This step should be done even if you have no immediate intentions to hang

yourself. Accidents may happen in the next step. Once finished, resume the exact position taken in Step 6.

8.  Jump off the chair or have your friend crawl quickly out of the room. Clutch wildly at your throat. Eventually give up and search for the chair or long-gone friend with your dangling feet. Spasm. (Do not give up. This part can be quite tricky, so be patient.) Attempting to scream and bugging your eyes out will do little good, though they are common occurrences in this situation. After some time, stop breathing and violently void your bowels onto the floor. You should have placed a courtesy towel beneath your hanging spot, but it will probably be too late for that at this point.

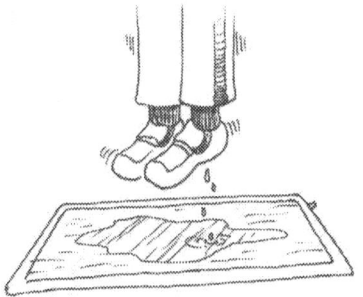

Though a gentleman knows that *please* and *thank you* are the "magic words," he does not believe in magic, and therefore, leaves such silly phrases to be used only by children and superstitious people.

When a gentleman is handed a nametag, even if it does not say his name, he proudly wears it on his lapel.

A gentleman never discusses his past, gives advice to others, or makes general statements about what it takes to be considered a gentleman.

A gentleman never rudely parks his car adjacent to any other vehicles. If this is impossible to avoid, he takes his business elsewhere. If his business cannot be taken elsewhere, he gives his car to the first homeless person he can find.

A gentleman honks his car's horn whenever a bumper sticker instructs him to do so. Aside from that, he only uses the horn to entertain his passengers with some of his heavily-practiced car horn show tune medleys.

A gentleman can easily sew on a button. But he can also sew flaps of human flesh together, whether it is to close a bleeding wound or close a running mouth.

A gentleman purchases at least one newspaper every day, preferably the *Wall Street Journal*, for the sole purpose of recycling it as soon as possible to help heal the environment.

# 2

# The Immaculate Gentleman Who Is Able to Dress Himself

A gentleman is ridiculously tidy. The dirtiest object a gentleman will put in his mouth is his own penis, which of course is scrubbed with bleach 3 times each day.

A gentleman realizes the importance of having hands that are much softer than any virginal maiden's hands. To achieve such supple skin, he soaks his hands in scalding motor oil for a minimum of two hours each day.

If a gentleman comes down with the slightest bit of a cold, he promptly shuts himself in his house and bleeds himself with leeches until he either recovers or passes away.

Since all nudity is tasteless and vulgar, a gentleman is never naked, even while bathing alone.

In order to look presentable at all times, a gentleman duct tapes his undershorts to his waist and staples his undershirt to his chest.

Keeping too many objects in a gentleman's pockets may ruin his slacks. If a gentleman feels it necessary to carry so many objects, he rips the pockets out of his trousers and acquires an attractive, yet sensible purse.

A gentleman ties his own shoes. Especially if they are hi-tops. Especially if they are bright red. Especially if Mommy says he has to.

A gentleman plucks any unsightly nose hairs, regardless of whether they are in his own nose. He does the same to his toenails.

# The Scent of a Gent

A gentleman uses cologne if he notices that he possesses unpleasant body odors, though he exercises caution in doing so. To avoid using an excessive amount, a gentleman dilutes his bottle of cologne with an offensive-smelling liquid that is equal in strength to the cologne. This concoction perfectly neutralizes all odors surrounding the gentleman. A few drops on either cheek, a teaspoon in his underpants, a splash on the inside of each elbow, and the remainder of the bottle soaked into his handkerchief should serve its purpose well.

When a gentleman feels that he needs to dye his facial hair, he understands that this is a low-class thing to do. Instead, he shaves some Japanese symbols into his beard and pierces a painful part of his face.

A gentleman strives to avoid having dandruff, which can only be done by acquiring the assistance of the Dandruff Wizard.

If a gentleman is inclined to wearing extravagant hats—such as silly Dr. Seuss stovepipe hats or hats with wacky slogans about excessively drinking alcohol—he understands that he will be the life of any party.

A gentleman never wears a belt if he can afford some rope.

Wearing one top-hat is mandatory.
Wearing two top-hats is polite.
Wearing three top-hats is excessive.
Wearing four top-hats is perfectly elegant.

# A Gentleman Covers His Head

Every gentleman has a healthy stockpile of top-hats, which he wears whenever he goes anywhere that he might encounter people. This includes attending the theatre, participating in organized sports events, and performing construction work. Though at times a gentleman may feel that his top-hat is an extension of his body, he should never forget that a hat is a hat and not a human body part. Therefore, he treats the hat as it should be, as a clothing accessory that is made to sit atop a person's head.

Following the traditions of the past two centuries, a gentleman removes his hat whenever he is being introduced to his parents or whenever he is in the presence of an individual who is widely considered to be a divine being, like William Shatner or a third-grade teacher. If a gentleman happens to be wearing his cap to hide an open head wound or another smaller cap which he has just stolen, he refrains from removing it. Instead, he opts to remove one of his shoes and uses it to pantomime the action of respectfully removing his hat. This simple gesture is pleasant, polite, and depressing all at once.

When a gentleman wears his clip-on black bow tie with a T-shirt, he always tucks the tie completely inside his shirt collar. This way, the T-shirt will help disguise the fact that the bow tie is a clip-on.

If a gentleman wears a cummerbund, he makes sure to carry a can of mace or a handgun because he knows that criminals will immediately try to make off with his precious cummerbund.

A gentleman always allows his underpants to air out overnight before he puts them back on in the morning. The same rule applies for his condoms.

Gentlemen need not feel guilty if they forget to wear their penny loafers after Memorial Day. Gentlemen in the south, of course, are never required to wear penny loafers, much less any other type of shoe or clothing. As a matter of fact, Southern gentlemen may disregard half of the content in this book.

# Tuxedo Time for Gentlemen

A gentleman never dons his tuxedo before six o'clock in the morning, unless he is being paid or slightly pressured to do so. This rule is also void if the gentleman is dressing up as a gentleman for Halloween. If a gentleman is renting his dinner clothes—which is the proper term for a tuxedo—he gets as much wear out of it as he can before he must return it.

If a gentleman receives an invitation to a "black tie event" or a party where "a black tie is optional," he wears a black tie and nothing else, though whether or not it is a bow tie is ultimately up to him. Dressing in such a manner is called "wearing your birthday suit."

A gentleman's "church-going suit," which is carefully tailored one size too small in order to direct the attention of single young ladies to his crotch area, may be worn to any party in which there is no dress code specification. However, he should carry his dinner clothes and birthday suit to the party just in case he may have misread the invitation.

Unless he can locate the state of Texas on a map or has no sense of fashion whatsoever, a gentleman does not wear cowboy boots.

If the weather is chilly, a gentleman wears thick gloves. No one appreciates a cold handshake. However, everyone appreciates a cold milkshake. Because of this, the gentleman fills his gloves with a milkshake flavor of his choice before he puts them on.

As long as there is no fingernail polish used, a gentleman may indulge himself in a manicure from time to time. When no one is looking, he may also enjoy a pedicure. Regardless of who is watching or what beauty products are involved, a gentleman may give himself a genicure, which is a thorough cleansing and massaging of his genitalia.

# The Paradox of Brown Shoes

In the complex hierarchical system of shoe color importance, black shoes are regarded as the king. As far as shoe type is concerned, loafers are at the top of the ladder. Brown is just barely inferior to black; penny loafers are ever-so-slightly less powerful than loafers. The color white and tennis shoes are much further down the list. Sandals and the color purple are barely acceptable as footwear.

A pair of serious, regal, and unswerving black loafers tells the world that business is about to be conducted by a shrewd gentleman. Following the same logic, a pair of black penny loafers appears far more intimidating on the basketball court than a pair of white sneakers.

However, situations happen and choosing the most powerful combination of shoe color and type is not always possible. For instance, if a business-minded gentleman insists upon wearing brown or salmon-colored suits, or if his driveway is particularly muddy, a nice pair of brown galoshes may better fulfill his needs. Another gentleman who is unemployed and homeless might prefer to wear any kind of shoe-like objects that fit on his feet and keep him from having his flesh torn by rusty nails and shards of glass.

A gentleman wisely invests in the fanciest dancing shoes that he can find since he knows that they, and only they, are the secret to good dancing.

When wearing a double-breasted suit, a gentleman should entertain his companions with an amusing joke about the juxtaposition of men's double-breasted suits and women's double-scrotumed skirts.

A gentleman's pants cuffs are where he stores his pennies, sentimental photographs, penny loafers, and emergency pairs of clean socks.

A gentleman's socks are shined as brightly as his shoes.

When a gentleman wears a vest, he knows that he is one step closer to becoming a full-time ninny.

As needed, a gentleman resoles his shoes with cardboard, aluminum foil, Styrofoam, or any other environment-friendly materials.

A gentleman owns at least one black lace teddy.

If a gentleman rents his dinner clothes, he understands that such crude behavior has not been considered socially acceptable since biblical times.

When a gentleman gains weight and can no longer fit into his clothes, he dismantles the clothes and builds bigger clothes from the pieces. If he is too lethargic to do this, he throws his clothes away and embarks upon a day-long shopping spree. If he finds that he cannot afford this, he rummages through the garbage cans of his wealthy overweight neighbors for hand-me-downs.

A gentleman does not dye his hair. He may, however, "frosts his tips" and "get his nails did."

Although a gentleman usually entrusts a laundromat with his shirts, he also knows how to scrub them clean on large rocks in the river.

A gentleman never eats bow tie pasta while wearing a bow tie, unless his bow tie happens to be a piece of uncooked bow tie pasta.

A gentleman never wears the same pair of blue jeans twice. This is one of many reasons why life as a cowboy gentleman is harder than that of, say, a pirate gentleman or an aborigine gentleman.

A gentleman's pants are always pleated except for that pair of pants he never wears because they are made out of poisonous radioactive materials.

If a gentleman's pants are not pleated, he may iron pleats into his pants to give them a more pleated look. In case of an emergency, artificial pleats may be purchased at any 24-hour convenience store.

# 3

# A Gentleman's Dining Habits

A gentleman eats the garnish before his entrée because garnish has an unpleasant appearance.

After business hours, a gentleman does not carry a disembodied head into a restaurant, even if it is his date for the evening.

A gentleman is never hesitant to fill out a restaurant's comment card with negative criticisms if he had an unpleasant experience there. He keeps this card, however, and when he returns to the restaurant, he reads it loud enough so that all of the wait-staff, management, line cooks, and his fellow patrons may hear of his previous tribulations.

# A Gentleman's Tipping Habits

Tipping is not a dinner topic. It is a private matter that a gentleman settles with his server in as discreet a manner as possible. A gentleman should never reveal the size of his gratuity, even to the man or woman who just served him.

Good service is rewarded by leaving a tip of at least 25 percent of the total bill. If this is beyond the gentleman's price range, he instead leaves 15–20 percent of his meal uneaten for his server to enjoy after he is gone. If the gentleman feels the service was lacking, he may demand a reverse-gratuity of 10 percent from the server or 15 percent from the management. In any case, a gentleman is sure to leave a nickel on the table, not only as a symbol of good luck, but also as a reminder that, at least in America, very few products and services are worth more than a nickel.

If a gentleman is served his meal first, which should always be done to ensure a high quality of food service, he refuses to eat until all others at the table have finished their meals. If his companions refuse to begin eating until he does, the gentleman finds another table at which to dine.

If a gentleman is trying out a new diet, he does not participate in it while eating with others, for fear of making them self-conscious about their own weights.

If a gentleman forgets to make dinner reservations at a restaurant, he uses the restaurant's drive-thru.

A gentleman spits out any food he was chewing before he speaks.

A gentleman knows that his salad fork is one of the forks beside his plate. If the fork he chooses to use as his salad fork is not the correct one, he makes a big scene, insulting the servers and attempting to get his meal discounted.

When a gentleman is done eating, he imagines his plate to be the face of a clock and arranges his knife and fork on it so as to signify the time that he finished eating.

Every time a gentleman dirties his dinner knife, he wipes it clean with the underside of the tablecloth.

A gentleman never insults the cook by salting his food before he tastes it, unless he plans on preserving that meal underground for next winter. Cooks aren't too sensitive about pepper usage, so it may be applied as liberally as he pleases.

# The Dinnerware Dilemma

Often confusing, but endlessly helpful, forks can make or break a gentleman's dining experience. It is the server's responsibility to make sure that each person at the table has a full set of dinnerware, but if the server fails to do this, the gentleman steps in.

Since each course uses one fork, one spoon, and one knife each, there should be as many of each as there will be courses in the meal. A typical meal has seven courses. If anyone at the table is lacking a piece of silverware, the gentleman provides them with a piece of his own. This means that he might have to make do with his fingers or any extra silverware at some points throughout the meal. A pair of heavy-duty gloves should be worn so that the gentleman's hands don't become dirtied with food.

# A Vegetarian, a Gentleman, and a Vegetarian Gentleman

Despite his own affinity for consuming the flesh of animals, a gentleman may one day wind up playing host to a misguided soul who prefers a strict meatless diet. The polite term for such a person is a vegetarian. If a gentleman questions his vegetarian guest and is satisfied with their reason for being a vegetarian (for instance, because it is less efficient to feed grain to a cow and then eat the cow, instead of just eating the grain and sharing some with the cow), he may go out of his way to prepare an enjoyable meal that is free from meats and dairy products. If the vegetarian is a vegetarian simply because they watched a disturbing propaganda video about the meat industry or if they have some sort of theory that equates the death of animals with the death of human beings, the gentleman may ridicule the person (as long as it is within his own house), he may prepare a bland and gross-looking vegetarian meal, or he may secretly slip meat and dairy products into the meal and pass it off as a "veggie meal."

If a vegetarian gentleman finds himself in the middle of a meat-eating situation from which he cannot escape without insulting his host or hostess, he pretends to eat the meat by holding the meat close to his mouth and making loud smacking sounds, followed by an audible gulp. Some hosts may not be fooled by this display, in which case the gentleman should force himself to deny his meatless belief system and actually eat the meat. He can always vomit up the fleshy tissue later, preferably in a place that is highly visible to the carnivorous guests and that is also difficult for his meat-eating hosts to clean.

If a gentleman ever comes across a person who eats only meat and no vegetables, he asks them for an autograph and buys them a steak.

When faced with the daunting task of a plate full of long pasta—such as fettuccine, spaghetti, or linguine—a gentleman resists the temptation to stuff his mouth full of noodles and pretend to be regurgitating a ball of worms that have infested his guts. Instead, he cuts each noodle in half with his knife (to make sure it is dead), curls it onto his spoon with his fork, and, still using all three utensils, carefully guides each noodle into his mouth.

A gentleman drinks his cocktails without the aid of a straw, which is reserved for soups, salads, and non-alcoholic cocktails.

# A Gentleman's Dinner Reservation Reservations

A gentleman handles all arrangements of his dinner outings, making reservations far ahead of time at a minimum of three restaurants to ensure that his party will be seated somewhere that night. If a gentleman's reservation gets declined because his dinner party is too large, he drops as many guests as is necessary for a reservation to be secured. When the night arrives and the restaurant refuses to seat the full party, the gentleman leaves the restaurant and reschedules the social dinner for another night at a different restaurant.

If his party has special requirements, like seating in a handicapped area or requesting an excessive number of booster seats, he expects his fellow dinner guests to handle their own nit-picky particulars.

Sometimes a hostess, manager, or maitre d' will be particularly helpful with acquiring the proper reservation, which the gentleman will acknowledge with a wink, kiss, and lingering handshake. He considers this friendly display to be his "tip" for a job well done.

A gentleman does everything in his power to avoid the list that all restaurants share between them which details the names and descriptions of customers who frequently miss their reservations. Once his name goes down on that list, the gentleman's business will not be appreciated and he will have to begin foraging for food in the woods.

# How to Order Wine All by Yourself

A gentleman orders the most expensive bottle of wine on the list, assuming that it has the best taste. If this wine is out of his price range, or if he is not fond of wine, he informs his dinner companions that they will be responsible for purchasing the evening's wine. He then drinks a glass of his companions' wine to show his respect for their taste in wine.

As a general rule, red wines compliment red foods like tomatoes, red meat, and red corn. White wines generally go best with white foods like ice cream, cauliflower, and white corn. All foods that do not fit into these two color categories may be accompanied by a nice cola-type beverage or light champagne.

When the gentleman's wine arrives, the server presents it to him and allows him to read the bottle's label. The gentleman pretends to do this. Then the gentleman is presented with the cork. Even if he's read the wine's label many times before, and even if he is allergic to cork and can't smell it, this is all done slowly and ritualistically so everyone at the table will anticipate the wine even more. Finally, the server pours a few drops of wine into the gentleman's glass. The gentleman swirls these drops around for a few seconds, counts backwards from 100 to 1, and tosses the glass over his left shoulder. Then and only then may the server retrieve a new glass for the gentleman and begin pouring the wine for everyone at the table.

The server will leave the bottle on the table or in a decorative basket underneath the table. The gentleman is free to wait for the server to return and refill his glass or he may perform the duties of the server and dispense the wine himself, first to other tables and then to his own.

When pouring a glass of wine, a gentleman catches any unsightly drips and dribbles with his tongue.

If a gentleman is dining in a restaurant and he recognizes some acquaintances sitting at another table, he hides his face with a menu or plate as he sneaks out of the restaurant, secretly paying for his acquaintances' check out of courtesy.

A gentleman never crunches ice cubes while in the presence of others, opting instead to hold each cube in his hand until it is fully melted and can be silently slurped up.

At the dinner table, a gentleman considers himself to be the guardian of the lady sitting to his right, which means he chooses menu items for her, converses only with her, and persistently offers to help remove her jacket.

# The Many Uses of a Dinner Napkin

Before he takes his seat, a gentleman asks his server if the restaurant performs some sort of amusing demonstration to celebrate the unfolding of the table napkins. If no such pre-dinner entertainment is being offered, he grabs his napkin and tucks one corner into his collar and the opposite corner into the front of his waistband. This transforms the napkin into both a hand cleaner and a food-catching bib. If the gentleman's hands are already dirty, he may politely order his server to do this for him.

If he is used to dining on placemats, a gentleman may remove his napkin and spread it out beneath his plate. The dinner napkin may also be used to save the gentleman's seat if he needs to leave the table during dinner. If the cook is being too liberal with his sauces or if the gentleman finds a disagreeable ingredient in his meal, he may use his napkin to get rid of whatever he needs. The dinner napkin may also function as an icebreaker (figuratively), a covering for one's plate, a hood, a miniature tablecloth, a makeshift receptacle in which to carry food home, an icebreaker (literally), and a doodle pad.

Even the most elegant of dinner parties may serve pick-up foods, like broccoli spears, tater tots, and crackers, all of which a gentleman may eat with his fingers. Chicken fingers, lady fingers, or any other finger foods with the word "fingers" in their name should be eaten with forks or toothpicks so as not to seem vulgar. Dipping sauces are nothing but trouble and should be avoided at all costs.

If a gentleman finds a leaf or seed has gotten lodged between his teeth, he turns his back on whomever he was chatting with and quickly digs the item out with the fingernail of his right pinky, which is left long and uncut for just such an emergency.

If a gentleman is attending a cocktail party or dinner and he realizes that he just put something rotten or poisonous into his mouth, he clumsily asks a fellow guest to hold a napkin in front of his head while he spits the foul substance into his shirt pocket. He might also choose to scrape his tongue clean using his fingers or salad fork.

In the rare instance that a gentleman chooses not to drink wine with his meal, he is sure to ingest a liquid that is equally as flammable, yet not as intoxicating, as alcohol. Ginger ale with a splash of lighter fluid or kerosene with a dash of cream are two acceptable alternative beverages.

If a gentleman absolutely has to answer his phone during dinner, he makes an extra spot at the table for the telephone and shoves some of his food into the phone's receiver so whoever is calling may enjoy the meal as well.

# 4

# The Social Gentleman

When he is complimented, a gentleman replies with a firm, "Ok." If someone tells him, "I like something about you," a gentleman does not feel worthy of their praise and does something despicable that makes them like him less. The only other option is handing the compliment-giver everything in his wallet, which may be done before the compliment is even said, which is known as purchasing the compliment outright.

If a gentleman phones an acquaintance and their answering machine picks up, he is sure to engage the machine in a friendly conversation.

When a gentleman wishes to excuse himself from a social gathering, he pretends to have diarrhea or the need to vomit. For added authenticity, he may wish to allow a small amount of feces or upchuck to spill out as he tightly clutches his rear end or mouth and rushes from the room.

If a gentleman's penis falls out of his trousers in the midst of a social situation, he tries to pass it off as a large, penis-shaped zipper for his trousers.

Arguing is not an option for gentlemen. If any person has an opinion about something, a gentleman faithfully accepts that person's opinion as his own truth. This is why the world is both round and flat.

A gentleman never feels the need to be nice to a person whom he considers to be unpleasant. If such a person insists on crossing the gentleman's path in some way, the gentleman may quickly and quietly attack them from behind. Some gentlemen prefer to offer the unpleasant person a firm and clearly-spoken warning a few seconds in advance of the attack. Regardless of his method, this is yet another reason for all gentlemen to carry at least one razor-sharp knife at all times.

# The Delicate Art of Beginning a Conversation

At parties, receptions, or business meetings, a gentleman attempts to strike up conversations with everyone he sees. He understands that most people like to converse only about banal or unimportant things. Therefore, he should start out with something like, "Boy, the weather sure is something, isn't it?" or "Do you mind if I have a conversation with you?"

If the person cordially acknowledges his presence or does not slowly back away from him, he asks a few more questions that he hopes will bring the conversation around to himself and his many fantastic accomplishments.

After a few minutes have passed, the gentleman may inquire about the person's name, age, and marital status. Never should the gentleman bring up sensitive and meaningful topics like philosophy or the latest sports statistics, unless he is sure that the person could be easily swayed to alter their religious beliefs or sports team affiliations.

# The Importance of Using Names to Address People

A gentleman understands that only personal friends address one another with their first names. Therefore, anyone whom he does not consider to be a close friend, regardless of whether he just met them, he addresses as "Mr." or "Ms." However, if Mrs. Taddersly tells the gentleman, "Please call me Cookie from now on," he immediately complies, referring to her as 'Ms. Cookie' from that moment forward.

If an acquaintance constantly refers to him as 'Mr. Baker,' the gentleman may rightly deduce that the person is unaware that the gentleman's last name is not Baker, but he still answers to Baker so as not to hurt the acquaintance's feelings. If he is often called "Mrs. Baker," the gentleman realizes that he is apparently ugly or effeminate enough to be mistaken for an older married woman. If he is frequently referred to as 'Ms. Baker,' the gentleman is proud that others consider him to be as lovely as an unmarried young lady.

# The Not-So-Delicate Art of Ending a Conversation

A gentleman knows that the responsibility of ending a conversation always sits upon his shoulders. Conversations adhere to a natural rhythm that goes a little something like this: beginning of discussion, a lengthy middle part, and then a pleasant fading out of the conversation. By mumbling and decreasing the volume of his voice in a gradual manner, the gentleman eases his companion(s) into a slow and gentle silence.

If the person asks the gentleman to speak up and quit mumbling as he does this, he knows that the conversation is not yet ready to end. Despite the number of confusing and uncomfortable pauses that may occur throughout the conversation, the gentleman does not let the discussion drop until he has successfully been able to fade it out in the relaxing manner described above.

Whenever he initiates a conversation with his telephone, a gentleman knows that he must be the one to end the conversation since the telephone is unable to hang itself up.

# A Gentleman's Stupid Mistakes

Though he strives for absolute perfection, a gentleman understands that sometimes facts can be misconstrued to make it appear that the gentleman has made a mistake. Some gentlemen may find that such misunderstandings occur quite often.

Therefore, all gentlemen would greatly benefit from creating a number of authentic-sounding apologies that can easily be tailored to fit specific circumstances. For instance, if a person claims to have been offended by a gentleman, he knows that they are merely being over-sensitive, yet he caters to them anyway by saying, "Peter, if I meant to seriously offend you when I described your pants as a corduroy nightmare, then I would be the fool here, but I don't think that I am."

If the gentleman's actions have gotten him into trouble because they were perceived by other less-than-perfect individuals, he attempts to smooth the situation over by saying something like, "At the Patterson's last Tuesday, Kay, I didn't accidentally burn a hole in your cheek with my cigar, you purposefully extinguished my tasty cigar with your face."

If he wishes to garner some pity for himself, a gentleman may compose an elaborate apology for a wrong that never existed. This way, he may gain the attention and respect from others, while having an apology ready and queued for the next time that he is accused of doing wrong.

A gentleman holds a grudge only if he feels that someone has wronged him in some way. He does not hold a grudge against those that he has wronged.

A gentleman mercifully accepts all apologies offered to him, unless the one offering the apology is a fellow gentleman. In this case, both gentlemen slowly back away from the spot in which they were chatting and wait for the perfect opportunity to exact their revenge upon one another.

If he means to say, "Excuse me," but instead says, "I'm sorry," a gentleman stops whatever it was he was doing and says, "Excuse me. I'm sorry that I said 'I'm sorry.' I meant to say 'Excuse me.'" If the person refuses to excuse him, he expresses further sorrow before excusing himself from the room.

# Kissing People in a Meaningless, Non-Romantic Way

A gentleman understands that some of his friends, co-workers, or customers may expect to exchange a social kiss with him whenever they greet him or leave his presence. Quick and fleeting, such kisses should signal to the gentleman that these individuals are sexually attracted to him.

If a woman initiates a social kiss by aiming her lips toward his cheek, the gentleman offers up his entire cheek and allows her to indulge in her fantasy. He may place his hand on the back of her head, lightly pressing the front of her face into the side of his own. The other hand may roam where it may on the woman's body, as long as it is out of the sight of any nearby children or elderly people.

If the woman leaves a smudge of lipstick on the gentleman's face, he does not immediately wipe it off with his sleeve. Instead, he asks the woman to leave a matching lipstick smudge on the opposite cheek. This draws less attention to the lipstick and keeps his face looking fairly symmetrical and well-moisturized.

# Composing Sympathy Notes As If You Really Do Care

If a gentleman learns that one of his acquaintances has passed away, he immediately sets out to convince the acquaintance's loved ones that he is saddened by the fact that all human beings must eventually die.

The gentleman's best bet is to make broad statements that express a melancholy attitude while simultaneously cursing the inevitability of death and decay. He might write, "I've been so depressed and immobile since Jason's brutal death, I lost my job and will probably have to go on welfare again. Curse you, death and decay!" Or he may wish to soothe his friend's anguish by writing, "I know that Jason meant a lot to you when he was alive. I hope that he still means something to you in the future, even though you will never again lay eyes upon his dead body, which is now buried so those of us who are living don't have to smell him as he decomposes."

Beyond writing them a touching note or two, a gentleman may offer to cook a fancy meal, run errands at the mall, or watch the grieving family's television while they attend the funeral.

# How to Lodge a Complaint and Mean It

At times, a gentleman may feel the need to burden someone else by complaining to them. If he feels somehow neglected, if he has been fatally wounded, or if he is terribly bored, he may rightfully choose to make his dissatisfaction publicly known.

Most complaints can be made to anyone who is willing or not willing to listen to them, such as a waiter, a volunteer paramedic, or a comatose vagrant. However, a gentleman knows that lurking in the shadows somewhere, there is a wily and cruel man named Mr. Bastard who is really the only person who needs to hear his complaints. Of course, it will never be possible to get in touch with Mr. Bastard, who constantly thwarts the gentleman's attempts to lead a happy and successful life. This situation in itself is reason for yet another complaint to be piled on top of the tall stack of complaints that the gentleman already possesses.

When it comes time to actually register the complaint with whatever poor clerk happens to be around when he's doing it, the gentleman is painstakingly specific about why he is complaining. He understands that he is on a quest to turn his displeasure into pleasure by conversely displeasuring someone else. If he cannot easily do this, he starts making wild and fantastic threats, the greatest of which is the threat of taking his business elsewhere.

A gentleman does not discuss his finances with other people, even his banker. He feels free, however, to share his financial woes or merriments with the friendly faces that adorn most forms of his country's currency.

If there are other people in the room speaking in an unfamiliar foreign tongue, a gentleman is careful not to let on that he is not fluent in their particular language. He understands that if he does this, he might provoke the barbaric foreigners into doing something terrible to him.

When a gentleman moves down the row in a crowded theater, he faces the screen or stage so he will not miss any of the show. He should only halt his movements if he sees that it is a really good part.

A gentleman does not bring his pets along when he runs errands or visits the homes of others unless his pets are Amazing Live Sea-Monkeys, or unless his errands involve delivering Amazing Live Sea-Monkeys around town, or unless the homes he plans on visiting are currently unoccupied.

# Mandatory Matrimony: A Gentleman Goes to Weddings

A gentleman attends every wedding that he hears of, regardless of whether or not he was invited. He makes sure to thoroughly and publicly humiliate any bride and groom who neglect to offer him an invitation. The easiest and most effective way to do this is by throwing a larger, more expensive wedding on the same day at a chapel that is as close as possible to the chapel of the wedding in which he was deliberately not invited.

If there is some kind of mix-up in the mail and a gentleman ends up being invited to a particular wedding, he remembers to sit on the right side of the chapel if he is rooting for the bride and the left side if he attended college with the groom. In the rare case that neither of these things are true, or if the gentleman is remotely related to either the bride or groom, he secures himself a cozy seat in the middle of the chapel's center aisle.

Throughout the ceremony, a gentleman attempts to stand and sit a few seconds before everyone else does, loudly clearing his throat as a cue for the other wedding attendees to sit or stand. Any time an instrumental song is played and a gentleman feels that he can provide appropriately passionate lyrics, he may croon loudly from his seat, enhancing the romantic atmosphere of the wedding. He never charges for this service, though he may pass his top-hat around for donations.

At the reception, a gentleman introduces himself with a handshake and kiss to everyone in attendance, including the wait-staff, the charming miniature couple atop the wedding cake, and whatever pleasant gentlemen he sees if he happens to walk by a mirror.

Gentlemen who chew tobacco must never allow another person to see them spitting or drooling their brown tobacco juice. Swallowing eliminates this problem. A tobacco chewing gentleman should also never complain when his teeth look like raisins and his bottom jaw rots off.

A gentleman ridicules those who are weaker and/or less fortunate than himself once they have passed well out of earshot. This rule, of course, does not apply to deaf or blind people since they either can't hear him or they can't find him to offer any physical retaliation.

A gentleman never makes idle threats. He always thoroughly illustrates his threats with diagrams and graphs, taking extra time to offer a small preview or question-and-answer session for the forthcoming threatened events.

A gentleman either brags that he never whines, or whines that he has nothing to brag about, but never both.

A gentleman tells amusing anecdotes about his lonesome and boring life whenever there is an awkward silence, even when he is not in the company of others.

A gentleman discusses his odorous pubic hair only if A) he is engaged in a conversation about them already, or B) he has nothing else to talk about.

If a gentleman is caught without breath mints for any reason, he either pretends that he has no tongue or avoids all conversation until he can locate a mint.

A gentleman understands that telephones were never meant to be used during times in which people may be enjoying their meals. Therefore, he restricts all of his personal phone activities to the hours between 1 AM and 4 AM.

A gentleman treats another person's dog as he would a dog of his own, feeding it handfuls of chili and harshly chastising it when it defecates all over the floor.

When a gentleman breaks wind in the presence of others, he quickly places his head as close to his anus as possible, inhaling deeply in an attempt to absorb all offensive gases.

If a gentleman somehow is entrusted to be a practicing physician who must carry a pager or cell phone with him at all times in case of emergencies, he is sure to leave the pager or phone with his secretary if he is going out for the evening. His secretary will, of course, follow him around throughout the evening, answering his phone or pager, offering his or her amateur prognosis, and prescribing medication at his or her own discretion.

# 5

# A Gentleman Abroad

If a gentleman arrives late to a cinema, he does not disturb other patrons with his tardiness. Instead, he waits patiently outside of the theater until the film's intermission or until the film ends, whichever comes first. While waiting, the gentleman should locate a friendly usher and discuss the most suitable place for him to sit in the auditorium. Once seated, a gentleman understands that his good behavior will catch the attention of a theater usher, who will later reward the gentleman with a small piece of candy or perhaps even a shiny nickel.

The first order of business to address when checking into a hotel or motel is befriending the local concierge. This can be done by purchasing the concierge an exquisite fur coat, by taking the concierge out for genuine "Italian Soda Waters," or by asking the concierge to circumcise the gentleman's first-born child.

It is a well-known fact that any bellhop can summon a cab faster than even the most charming gentleman could. Because of this, gentlemen never challenge bellhops to cab-summoning races. They do, however, tip bellhops who tipped them first.

A gentleman does not carry his cellular phone into a brothel, prison, carwash, or any other place where the ringing of his phone may distract or alert, and consequently annoy, others.

A gentleman refrains from picking his nose in public. He instead does it in private, promptly gobbling up whatever worthy morsels he finds therein.

# A Gentleman Goes to Market

A gentleman offers to count the number of items in other customers' grocery carts so they will know if they have exceeded the limit for entering the Express Checkout line. In return, the gentleman asks them to recount the items in his own cart so he does not make the same mistake. If someone offers the gentleman a spot ahead of them in line, he accepts and passes this act of kindness along by inviting the person at the back of the line to step in front of him.

If the cashier inquires about his preference of bag materials, the gentleman chooses whichever bags appear to be present in the greater quantity. As the cashier totals up his groceries, the gentleman may help those behind him in line unload their carts' contents onto the conveyor belt. Once that task is complete and it seems like everyone's items are arranged to provide the cashier with a series of quick and easy checkouts, he may then pay his bill and leave.

A gentleman abides by all public swimming pool rules except for the one that prohibits him from drowning other people because he plays too roughly.

A gentleman never eats gelatinous fruit snacks while he is behind the wheel of a vehicle, though he may sneak a few staples or paper clips while no one is looking.

For courtesy and safety reasons, a gentleman defends all automated teller machines with his life. If there is already a line of people waiting to use the machine, a gentleman assumes they are all criminals and tries to scare them away from the machine by setting it on fire.

A gentleman voids his bowels into a plastic baggy whenever he gets "the urge" at a friend's house. Dirtying the toilets of others is barbaric.

# A Gentleman Knows How to Fly

When traveling, a gentleman carries a spare empty suitcase to offer fellow travelers who do not have much luggage. If need be, he may store another person's smaller piece of luggage inside of the suitcase for more efficient space usage.

Since he shall be in very close quarters with the rest of the plane's passengers for perhaps hours, a gentleman bravely refrains from taking his seat until he has introduced himself to everyone onboard the flight. If a gentleman must use the restroom while in mid-flight, he occupies the restroom until the plane has safely landed and his excrement and/or urine are flushed from the plane's sewage reservoir.

A particularly thoughtful gentleman helps the stewards and stewardesses run a smooth operation by helping them serve the other passengers. Walking people to and from the restroom, serving meals to the plane's crew, and temporarily relieving the pilot of his duties so he or she might have a break are only a few of the many tasks that a gentleman should perform.

On long flights, say from Texas to Moscow, a gentleman may wish to entertain those flying with him by performing a classic Vaudeville song and dance routine that he learns specifically for such occasions. If he forgets to pack his red-and-white pinstripe jacket, straw hat, cane, and tap shoes, he may improvise with a stewardess uniform, the pilot's cap, a pack of peanuts, and his bare feet.

Though a gentleman should never create awkward silences, especially with strangers or children, some passengers may wish to handle business or sleep during the flight. The gentleman excludes such crass people from any full-contact sports games that he may organize as ice-breaker activities.

# A Gentleman, A Broad

A gentleman never makes a date with a below-average girl simply because he is feeling desperate. He should do so only if he is suicidal, horny, bored, or attracted to ugly girls with lame personalities.

A gentleman never refuses the sexual advances of any young lady, no matter what. Turning a lady down hurts her feelings, and a gentleman makes it his personal prerogative to keep every young lady from experiencing even one moment of loneliness or pain on this earth. This rule also applies to family members, dead ladies, and other gentlemen.

A gentleman may socialize, but not romantically date, with those outside of his species. Brief sexual encounters are the only exceptions to this rule.

If a gentleman is rejected when he asks to rape a young lady, he smiles and excuses himself, perhaps expressing his hopes of a future acceptance.

A gentleman never asks a young lady if she is pregnant, especially if he has recently ejaculated inside of her.

When on a date with a young lady, a gentleman opts to pick up the check for her meal only if he feels he may get the chance to *at least* fondle her breasts later.

A gentleman strives endlessly to procure a respectable young lady as his girl-friend, but doesn't waste valuable time worrying about what to do with her after he succeeds.

A last-minute date makes a gentleman seem spontaneous and exciting to be around. A good last-minute date is sneaking up behind a young lady, muffling her screams with a sock, placing her in the trunk of his car, and driving her to a very secluded (and therefore, very romantic) spot.

The only reason a gentleman breaks a date is if his date dies, and even then, only if the coroner denies him access to his date's corpse.

Even if a gentleman has been bitten by a werewolf and must feast on the raw meat of hapless victims every night, he still understands the importance of wearing a tuxedo while out on the town.

A gentleman never lets on that he is lost. When in doubt of where he is, a gentleman refers to a "map" that he carries with him at all times. This "map" is nothing more than an oversized piece of folded paper full of naughty doodles and useless diagrams.

A gentleman never fondles the children of others. He politely reserves that for the privacy of his own home.

When walking his dog, a gentleman refuses to allow his pet to crudely use the bathroom outside. An entire room in his house is designated for this hallowed and private activity.

A gentleman is perceptive. He notices if a person is in need of assistance and makes up polite-sounding excuses to get himself out of the bothersome tasks that they will surely ask of him.

# A Gentleman in Church

When attending a church that he's never seen before, a gentleman pretends to be quite familiar with the church's history, spiritual infrastructure, and cere-monial traditions. In order to convince others of his familiarity, he may offer stern corrections to those around him or he may assert himself as the church's leader.

In a church, opera, or other public gathering place, a gentleman knows to turn off all of his pagers, beepers, and cell phones, but only if he is 100% certain that he is not expecting any calls or pages.

It is a physical and logical impossibility for a gentleman to be late for a church service, but when he is, he makes sure to loudly and clearly inform the entire congregation of his reasons for being tardy.

# Grave Times: A Gentleman Goes to Funerals

At a funeral, a gentleman is sure to pay his respects. What this exactly means is a mystery, but it probably means that he is responsible for cheering everyone up. This can be accomplished by simply complementing his usual tuxedo with a silly hat.

In the case of a wake or viewing, a gentleman may use the corpse to entertain the audience with a brief ventriloquist act. The gentleman should only do this if he knew the corpse when it was alive.

A gentleman makes sure to out-mourn everyone else at a funeral.

Whenever a gentleman bothers other theater patrons by leaving his seat in the middle of a performance, he moves as quickly as he can through the aisle. If in his rush, he steps on someone's toes, he stops and allows them to step on his toes with twice as much accuracy and force.

If his automobile's turn signals do not work, a gentleman makes no turns when he drives.

If a gentleman must adjust his crotch while in public, he may do so by using the edge of a table or fencepost instead of his hands. If such things are not readily available to him, he may rub his crotch against the nearest person.

While waiting in line at the post office, a gentleman kindly allows every patron who walks in the door to step in front of him if they wish. He also checks the addresses on everyone's envelopes and packages in case they are mailing something to him.

# A Gentleman Works Out

A gentleman brings his own workout bench and set of weights to the gym.

If a gentleman suspects that he might have athlete's foot, he is sure to make all other users of the gym's bathroom aware by posting signs around the gym that read, "There is a good possibility that you will catch athlete's foot here." It is considered good form for the afflicted gentleman to also include a headshot of himself, as well as a picture of his bleeding and infected feet.

While in the gym, a gentleman carefully studies the physiques of each man he sees, offering compliments to those who are worthy and critical suggestions to those whom he considers to be less than perfect.

A gentleman does not shave in the gym shower, though he may urinate as he pleases as long as he soaks it up with his own washrag. He may then safely squeeze the soiled washrag into the nearest toilet.

# 6

# The Partying Gentleman

A gentleman accepts every invitation he receives. Turning down an invitation is like willfully contracting a face-disfiguring disease.

If a gentleman is the first to arrive to a party, he makes sure that he is also the last to leave.

If a gentleman throws a party and one of the guests breaks something of his, the gentleman refuses payment for it. If a gentleman breaks something at a party he is attending, he completely and immediately replaces the object. In the case of a gentleman breaking a gentleman's object at a party, there shall then be a Gentleman Standoff in which both gentlemen compliment each other mercilessly until one relents.

If a gentleman attends more than three bar mitzvahs or bat mitzvahs in his lifetime, he considers himself a certified Jew and publicly circumcises himself right away.

While in synagogue, if someone offers a yarmulke to a gentleman, he pretends to wear it by holding it very close to the top of his scalp.

When invited to a mustard party, a gentleman always brings yellow mustard, ketchup if he wishes to make a light-hearted joke, but *never* dijonnaise.

In the middle of a heated barroom brawl, a gentleman uses a broken beer bottle on his opponents *if and only if* a majority of his opponents are males. If a majority of them are females, he uses nothing smaller than nun-chucks.

Hosting frequent and ridiculously elaborate "pet parties" is not only an adorable and clever way to impress a gentleman's friends and neighbors, but it also provides everyone's pets with the opportunity to just unwind for once and mingle with some other fantastic pets.

If a gentleman finds that he has the tendency to lean back in his chair, he purposefully leans *way* forward in his chair.

# What to Do With an Invitation

A gentleman responds to every party invitation with a lengthy letter that includes the following: a detailed analysis of his upcoming personal schedule and all possible obstacles that might interfere with his ability to attend the party, any speculations or expectations he has for the party, a list of people and foods that he hopes to see at the party, and his entire self-written collection of tips and strategies for throwing fun and successful parties. The gentleman then writes letters to all of his friends and extended family members, inviting them to the party so they can share in his good fortune.

If an invitation is marked with the letters RSVP (an acronym for the name of a popular French restaurant chain), the gentleman knows that he should immediately attempt to book a flight to Paris and reserve a hotel room that is within two blocks of the RSVP.

If the gentleman regrettably has inescapable prior engagements, he asks the person if they can reschedule their party. If this is not possible, he must decline the invitation altogether.

The gentleman tries to cushion the blow of this blatant rejection either by dazzling the person with fascinating tales about his conflicting engagements or by confusing the person and running away. He might create interesting excuses like, "I will be enjoying my exotic vacation prize package that I won on a televised game show last night," or "My grandparents are treating me to five dollars' worth of gaming at the local arcade that night," or "I have stuff to do."

To confuse the person so that he can make a clean getaway, he might say, "I'm sorry that you can't attend my party. I will keep praying for you," or "Why, I thought your party was last week! That's why I threw my party last week," or "I'm not that type of bastard. But have a good party anyway."

If an invitation is marked "Regrets only," a gentleman sends the host or hostess a list of every event in his life that he has ever regretted.

Invitations use a very strict vocabulary to state the party's dress code. "Casual" means to wear whatever you happen to be wearing on that particular day, unless it is a business-casual outfit. "Business casual" suggests that no casual clothing may be worn. "Semi-formal" means to bring a date and wear a corsage. "Black tie" requires a felt-brimmed top-hat, a tuxedo with tails, a sweater vest (but not sweaters or vests), a belt, a decorative belt buckle, a modest-looking garter belt, and, of course, freshly polished suede loafers. A black tie is optional. "White tie" is a code word from the Ku Klux Klan handbook that means the party will be a gathering of white supremacists, so he needs to wear identity-concealing clothing and all of his blatantly racist regalia.

If a gentleman must decline an invitation that he has already accepted or if he wishes to reaccept an invitation that he had previously declined, he finds some way to do it without bringing it to the attention of the party's host or hostess.

# A Gentleman Posing as Bartender

Since a gentleman wouldn't mind having all of his alcohol sucked away by his greedy houseguests and their friends, he keeps his bar stocked with a wide variety of tasty beverages. To please the most discriminating of guests, he purchases at least one liquor of each color available, along with ice, water, and if he lives in the South, unsweetened iced tea mix.

A thrifty gentleman knows how to add water (and food coloring, if necessary) to his bottles when they are beginning to look a bit drained. If the gentleman has quite a few alcoholic friends, he may need to purchase the cheaper brands of liquor so he may feed their addiction with ample amounts of booze, which is all they will care about anyway.

Of course, a gentleman knows that no bar is complete without a variety of citrus fruits, a few sharp knives to slice the fruit with, toothpicks, straws, tiny umbrellas (to place in the straws), a milkshake machine, a whorish-looking bartender, and a tall stack of buttered, syrupy pancakes.

If a gentleman's answering machine contains a number of invitations, he waits until the machine is completely filled with invitations before deciding which one he will accept. It is rude to respond to an invitation if there is a remote possibility of other invitations appearing in the near future.

At a party, a gentleman assumes that everyone wants to meet him. Therefore, within the first five minutes of his arrival, he introduces himself to every person he can find, even those with whom he is already familiar.

If a gentleman receives an invitation that is addressed to him "and guest," he realizes that the party will be composed of himself, one other person, and the host, which could turn out to be quite a lame situation indeed. Therefore, he declines the invitation.

# Conforming with Other Party Guests

Even though most people consider a party to be a time for overindulgence in food, drink, and laughter, a gentleman does none of these things. He understands that he is only there to fulfill his duties as a guest, which include: to be entertained, to meet new people, and to be another moderate consumer of the host's food and drink.

If a gentleman does not arrive at the party precisely when it begins, then he knows that he has no business being there. He may still attend the party, but he cannot participate in any party activities or games. Nor can he enjoy any of the party snacks or beverages. Dancing and talking are not off limits, as long as the gentleman does these things by himself.

As the night comes to an end, the gentleman slowly, gracefully exits the party, shamelessly showing gratitude to his host or hostess by weeping and gnashing his teeth as he leaves.

If the gentleman is offered second helpings of a dish, he politely asks if he may have seconds. Regardless of the answer, however, he knows better than to ever partake of the seconds.

A gentleman always sits on a coaster.

In the powder room, a gentleman may use the hand towel to lightly blot or dry his hands and face, but only if they are not wet or dirty.

If a gentleman is not able to dance very well, he is content with walking briskly around the dance floor, alone or hand-in-hand, depending on whether or not he has a partner.

# Proper Gift-Giving Etiquette

A gentleman never enters the home of another without some sort of gift in his hands. If he is attending a dinner party, he brings a framed picture of himself or he brings another dinner (uncooked, so the host or hostess understands that the dinner is not meant to be eaten with the dinner at hand). For holiday parties, he may take a tin of stout mayonnaise, a jar of raw turkey giblets, some McFrondle's Holiday Value Coupons, a bottle of warm eggnog, or a bag of live crawfish.

If he will be enjoying an extended visit—overnight or until he finds a job—the gentleman's gift is more sizeable, such as a Salad Shooter, an extra ceiling fan, or an adorable house pet.

The gift should be ceremoniously presented to the host or hostess upon his entrance and exit of the hospitable residence. In the meantime, he cleverly hides thank-you notes around the house.

If a gentleman cannot afford to take a gift to a party, he takes a large box and secretly places one of the other guests' presents inside the box. He then wraps the big box with any wrapping material he can find, such as toilet paper or a scarf and then marks the gift as being from himself and the other guest.

# Making a Good Toast (Without Using Any Bread!)

Every gentleman should expect to be invited to a ridiculously large number of weddings, anniversary celebrations, birthday parties, funerals, and other traditional social gatherings. The rules of probability tell us that there is a very good chance that at least one of the millions of gentlemen in the world will be asked to make a toast during one of the billions of parties that will surely take place in the future. Thus, all gentlemen should be prepared to make a short, emotionally-packed toast at any moment.

The one and only toast he ever needs to memorize is this: "This is my toast to you, _____ (insert toastee's name here). My glass is raised. Everyone is being very quiet, except for me, because I am making this toast. When I am done with this toast, I expect everyone to laugh, smile, or lightly applaud. Then we shall all clink glasses with one another and take sips of our beverages. Then we can move along and be done with this contrived social expression of our admiration for _____ (again, insert toastee's name here). This is the end of my toast."

A gentleman helps clean up after every party he attends or hosts, getting a head start on the cleaning minutes after the party officially begins.

A toast is not complete until a gentleman has clinked glasses twice with everyone in the room (just to be sure the toast is effective).

If a gentleman lifts an empty glass while a toast is being made, he realizes that he is not rightfully participating in the toast. In order to do so, he must either slyly switch glasses with a fellow toaster or he must spit into his glass and then drink it.

A gentleman allows the bartender at a private party to serve him drinks as if he were a typical bartender working in a nightclub. He does not attempt to steal the bartender for his own private party and he also does not try to convince the bartender to leave and begin working at a more populated establishment.

A gentleman takes great pride in his ability to prepare a dinner by himself. He makes this known to his guests by way of a formal announcement and toast before he begins his preparations. If he gets lonely in the kitchen while his guests are having fun in the other room, he may ask for assistance with small tasks like mopping the floor or preparing the dinner.

A gentleman always sets the table at least one day prior to his guests' arrival. He also flushes the toilet well beforehand, throws away any trash his guests might need to dispose of, and buys gifts for himself so his guests will not feel pressured to do so.

Whenever alcohol is being served, a gentleman assumes that others will over-indulge. He is left with two options here: 1) Being the one who overindulges the most so others won't feel as bad, or 2) Constantly reminding others about the consequences and dangers of alcohol overindulgence with a hand puppet show.

# How to Tell People How to Sit at a Table

Few gentlemen have gone through life without being expected to "seat" a table of their friends. Such gentlemen were either hideous enough to have no friends or they couldn't afford a table at which to seat anyone. Unlike these wretched creatures, all normal, fortunate gentlemen get to enjoy the delightful task of arranging which of his guests should sit where. This situation is similar to the biblical concept of God creating the universe, and it should be treated just as seriously.

First, the gentleman holds a raffle among his guests to see who will be the Guest of Honor. This is done by taping a golden ticket underneath one of the chairs at the table. After he tells all of his guests to have a seat, he asks everyone to get up and look under their seats for a surprise. Whoever finds the ticket is the Guest of Honor and he or she will be seated first. A gentleman can never be the Guest of Honor since he always takes the least desirable seat in the house, which is usually one of the toilets.

After the Guest of Honor is crowned, inaugurated, and seated, the gentleman randomly selects the rest of the seating order by drawing tiny caricatures of his guests, putting the caricatures into his top-hat, and then wearing the top-hat. The seating order is determined by the order in which the caricatures fall out of his hat. A gentleman should wear his loosest top-hat on such occasions. This seating procedure ensures that no bias has clouded the gentleman's judgment and it is also guarantees a table full of handsomely entertained guests.

# How to Identify Dinnerware

A gentleman sets his table with instruments and gadgets that look similar to the ones pictured below and in the *exact* orientation shown below:

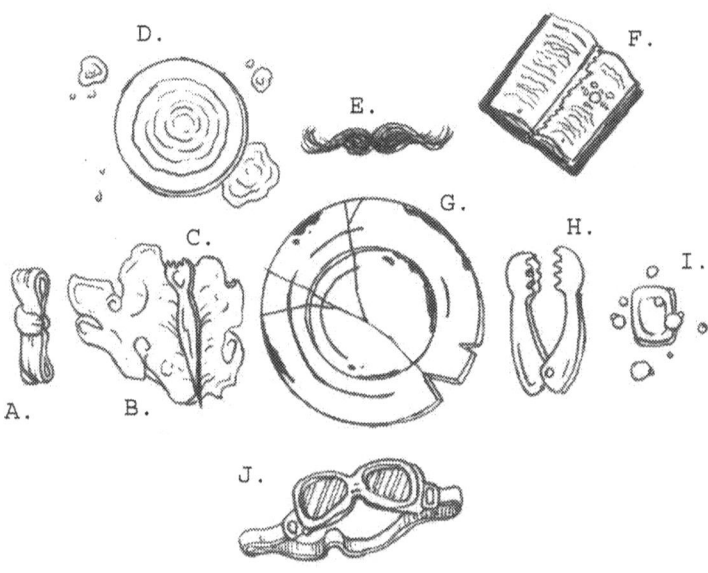

A. Spare bowtie
B. Well-used snot rag
C. Spork (with knife tip)
D. Water dish
E. His father's fake mustache

F. *The Semi-Complete Guide to Sort of Being a Gentleman*
G. The lowest quality plate he owns
H. Salad tongs
I. Moist bar of soap
J. WWII aviator goggles

# How to Pretend That You Know How to Serve Dinner

Before the gentleman will allow his guests to enter the house, all of the dinnerware must be placed on the table. He then lets the guests come inside and shepherds them toward the dining room. From there, the following procedure is carried out:

- The guests are seated by using the previously outlined seating method.

- The gentleman wheels the dessert cart around the table in a counterclockwise rotation, stopping just long enough for each guest to get a good peek at its tasty treats.

- The gentleman makes sure that all of his guests are hungry and intend on eating the dinner he is about to serve.

- The salad, appetizers, main course, and side dishes are all served in whatever order they come out of the microwave.

- The meal continues until all plates are emptied of their food and all glasses are drained of their fluids. The gentleman may make a few more quick passes with the dessert cart as he waits for his guests to finish.

- The dessert cart makes one final sweep around the table and comes to a permanent stop so its sugary contents may be unloaded into the guests' bottomless stomachs.

If the guests still feel like wasting more of the gentleman's time and electricity by chatting long after the plates and such have been thrown away, the gentleman ushers everyone into the living room, claiming that he has something incredible to show them. Once there, he begins yawning and pretending to fall asleep, at which point most of his guests will get the point that it is time to leave or take a big group nap on the living room floor.

# A Gentleman's Stockpile of Thank-You Notes

A gentleman purchases thank-you notes in bulk. Even for events such as birthday parties or potluck dinners, in which the gentleman also had to bring flowers or a gift, he needs to show his gratefulness with at least one thank-you note. (The flowers say, "I appreciate you," (because they are robotic talking flowers), but the thank-you note says, "Thank you," (though not out loud because it is just a piece of ordinary paper). The point here is that the two thank-you messages are different.)

If the evening was unpleasant or dull, the note might say, "Thank you for having me over, though I wish that I had squandered that evening at someone else's residence instead." Or he might say, "Thank you for giving me some of your food. The chemicals in it helped me survive for another day."

If he does not receive a you're-welcome note within a reasonable amount of time, the gentleman sends another, more compellingly-written thank-you note. After the fifth time he sends such a note, he drops it and moves on with his life.

A gentleman is never boring or bored at a dinner party. This remains true as long as he remembers to bring a portable video gaming device with him everywhere he goes.

At private parties that provide valet parking, a gentleman waits his turn and then allows the parking attendant to sit in his backseat. After parking his car, the gentleman opens the car door for the parking attendant and walks him back to his post. As he hands his keys over to the attendant, he slips a "tip" into the attendant's breast pocket. This "tip" is a blank, folded dollar-sized slip of paper.

A gentleman always keeps a few extra dollars in his pocket just in case he runs across any other gentlemen who need tip money. Any gentleman who borrows money for tipping purposes makes sure to tip the gentleman who gave him the tip money. A gentleman should never feel ashamed of asking others for money because his wallet was recently overwhelmed with too many tip-worthy people.

A gentleman does not throw BYOB parties unless the second "B" stands for "Babies."

If a gentleman procrastinated and is faced with sending out party invitations at the last minute, he respects his friends' busy schedules and does not put them in the mail. This might mean that nobody will know when and where to show up for his party, but at least the gentleman will still have his friends' admiration.

# A Gentleman's Duties as Host

Whether he is hosting a social gathering in his own home or in a restaurant, a gentleman is sure to provide the proper amount of entertainment for his guests. The best way to do this is with a television set and a party platter of potato chips and fancy cheeses. At all times of the day or night, television offers channels upon channels of satisfying entertainment options for party guests to enjoy, and a gentleman knows this. A gentleman who procures digital cable will soon become notorious for throwing the nicest parties and keeping his guests thoroughly entertained.

Gentlemen who have no television sets or only a few non-cable TV stations must resort to more fantastic forms of entertainment, such as extravagant street magic shows, impromptu wrestling matches with his furniture, or extreme motorcycle racing. He accepts any broken bones or bloody noses as unavoidable parts of entertaining his company.

Any unexpected dishes or bottles of wine that his guests bring are to be immediately consumed in their entirety by the gentleman.

A gentleman always offers to make coffee for any company he is entertaining in the morning time, but usually he "forgets" this and secretly pours himself a bowl or two of cereal.

When a gentleman is ready for his guests to leave, he keeps it to himself and settles on staring coldly at them and sighing loudly.

The invitations to a gentleman's party, whether they are done by telephone or by written announcement, give just enough information so people may find the place where the party is being held. All other details, like dress requirements, food and drink offerings, and the time and date of the party itself, are kept secret because people love surprises.

If a guest offers to prepare a dish or bring a bottle of wine, a gentleman makes a big production of praising that guest in front of the other guests so they will be more inclined to also help with the hassles of hosting the party.

A gentleman host uses his good china to serve only himself, serving all other guests with plastic disposable dinnerware. This way, there are no hurt feelings or broken friendships because someone accidentally broke a piece of his expensive china. Also, since he is going to be the only one using it, the gentleman is required to buy only one set of china.

Sometimes, a gentleman realizes that he has accidentally invited a rude or disagreeable person into his home. If he does not want the police to get involved in the removal of such a person, the gentleman sneakily organizes the other guests into a lynching party.

When hosting an intimate dinner party of only one or two guests, a gentleman is sure that he never rudely allows his guests to leave his sight. He invites them to follow him into the kitchen or bathroom so the conversation may continue while he finishes baking the salad or urinating.

# A Gentleman on Drugs

After snorting cocaine off the belly of a hooker who is in a heroin-induced coma, a gentleman always remembers to clean up any blood, vomit, etc., that might escape from the hooker's mouth or nose.

A gentleman always screens his calls for cops or angry drug-dealing pimps.

A gentleman gladly shares his needles with those who are in need of them.

A gentleman neither reads nor writes crude words. Especially not "donkey nut-shit fuckface." And especially not dime store fantasy novels about lonesome and naughty nursing home patrons.

# 7

# A Gentleman's Buddies

A gentleman does whatever he can to make other people feel superior to him. If he has problems with being exceptionally handsome, fit, or intelligent, he should disfigure himself, eat more fat-laden food products, and stop reading books and start watching television.

A gentleman assumes that no one in the world can meet any other person in the world without his assistance. A gentleman imagines that without people like himself introducing everyone, his parents may have never met and he wouldn't have been born. This pushes him to introduce even harder.

A gentleman jumps up and stands whenever he sees or hears people being introduced to each other.

If a gentleman sees that another gentleman has forgotten to zip his fly, he attempts to discreetly toss a nearby object into the gentleman's open zipper to alert him.

# How to Introduce People to People

Even though nobody remembers any of the old fashioned traditions of social introductions, a gentleman should pretend that he *does* remember them. Unless he can think up any better rules, he should adhere to the following:

- An older person, who has less time left on earth and, in general, has less to be happy about, should be introduced *to* a younger person, who is likely not even interested in meeting the older person. For instance, a gentleman would introduce Biff Garples, who is four, to Old Man Hurlipons, who is ninety-eight, by saying, "Biff, this is Old Man Hurlipons. He's going to die soon, so meet him while you can." Polite traditions such as this help old people feel that they are slowly walking ancient treasures.

- When introducing a man and woman who share the same age, a gentleman introduces the *woman* first. For instance, if Old Man Hurlipons and Esther Franiel do not know of each other, a gentleman would say, "Old Man, this is Esther Franiel. I said, Esther. No, not mustard spaniel. And not bastard Daniel. Ah screw it." Then he turns to Esther and says, "Esther, this is Old Man Hurlipons. No, Esther, he is not your daughter. Put your clothes on, Esther. Nurse, can we please sedate these two again?"

- A gentleman does all he can to stimulate a conversation between those he introduces. For example, he might say, "Biff, Old Man Hurlipons was once imprisoned for kidnapping a child. Tell Mr. Hurlipons why you don't talk to strangers." Or, "Esther, you've been living in the same room as Mr. Hurlipons for ten years, ever since your family grew tired of dealing with your senility and abandoned you in this nursing home. That's nice."

- If a gentleman is not sure about the pronunciation of a name, he offers as many variations of the name as possible throughout the conversation until he finds one that he likes.

Though he may not even know the two individuals whom he is introducing to one another, a gentleman does all he can to force these two people into a hasty and awkward introduction. Once he has accomplished this, he may introduce himself to the two newly-introduced acquaintances.

# Putting Up with Alcohol-Free People

If a gentleman has a friend who does not find it necessary to momentarily escape their unbearable existence through excessive alcohol consumption, he attempts to enlighten the person by showing them the absolute fulfillment that they are forfeiting. The gentleman understands that there is likely a foolish and misguided reason for the person abstaining from alcohol, for instance, stodgy religious beliefs, previous addiction problems, or the misconception that alcohol has no nutritional value.

If a gentleman finds alcoholic beverages unappealing for any reason, he refrains from drinking, unless it is expected of him or unless he and his fellow non-drinkers are in the minority. In such instances, it is normal to say something like, "I normally don't drink because I am unable to digest alcohol and my body reacts violently to it, but if you want to mix a cocktail for me, I will gladly drink it."

# Shaking Hands with Other People

Unless he does not have hands or he knows a good number of handless people, a gentleman shakes hands with anyone he comes across in a social setting, whether he is in a convenience store, a public restroom, or a funeral. If a gentleman is particularly popular or friendly, he should walk around with one hand permanently extended in order to shake hands with as many people in the smallest amount of time possible. When meeting older people and dignitaries, the gentleman should shake hands first and *then* introduce himself if he is asked to do so.

A gentleman successfully executes a handshake by pumping his hand up and down, gripping the other person's hand, halting his pumping, and tightening his grip until the other person's knuckles turn a creamy shade of white. Then he lets go and continues about his business.

When meeting a woman, a gentleman uses one hand to gingerly guide the woman's hand toward his other outstretched hand. Then, instead of heartily pumping and gripping her hand like he would if she possessed male genitalia, he lightly massages her hand from wrist to fingertips. If she pulls her hand away quickly, a signal that she does not wish to shake hands, the gentleman grasps her hand again and presses it tenderly to his lips.

Refusing to shake a person's hand is the most brutal insult a gentleman can muster. The only way a gentleman may rectify such an expression of rudeness and poor taste is by offering the offended person a double handshake (using both hands at once), a hug, a kiss, and a pleasant nod of his head.

A gentleman does not crash a party, unless it one that he is hosting.

When accompanying a woman across a crowded room—whether it is his daughter, his landlord, his doctor, his ex-girlfriend, or a transsexual client who is blackmailing him—a gentleman places both of his hands on her shoulders and firmly pushes her through the crowd, like steering an electric scooter.

A social engagement waits for no gentleman. If a gentleman finds that he is running late for a cocktail party or formal dinner, he stops along the way and orders a few drinks or a hamburger value meal, respectively, so that he will be caught up with the other party guests, who will surely have begun their merry-making without him.

# The Answer to Everything: Sending Flowers

A gentleman knows that sending flowers is appropriate for any conceivable occasion, such as the anniversary of a nasty break-up, a fictional character's birthday, a needless holiday like Lincoln Day or Christmas, a sudden lay-off, an abortion, or any other moment that either does or does not deserve a floral celebration. Flowers are the perfect way to thank grade school teachers of yesteryear for sacrificing the best years of their lives for the sake of educating hundreds of stupid, unappreciative children. On the contrary, flowers can be used to subtly tell a person that you refuse to put up with their abuse any longer or they can turn any regular old dirt garden into a better-looking flower garden. They may also function as a sweet and colorful dinner salad if no grocery stores are currently open.

However, a gentleman understands that there are certain times when flowers can be quite inappropriate. If a bereaved family requests that flowers not be sent to a funeral, the gentleman instead sends his flowers to the dead individual's former residence and helps gather up any flower bouquets that were inadvertently sent to the funeral home and cemetery anyway. A gentleman should only send flowers to his secretary if he recently fired her or if he is having an awkward affair with her.

Lastly, a gentleman always sends a tasteful corsage to his Homecoming dates, friends in prison, or other gentlemen.

# A Gentleman Housed as a Guest (a.k.a., a Gentleman as a Houseguest)

When staying as a guest in someone's home, a gentleman respects his host's furniture and other items as if they are his own and he does not want anything bad to happen to them. Covering the furniture with plastic tarps and carefully wrapping up any breakable objects, the gentleman thoroughly secures any room that he might be occupying.

A gentleman rewards any servants within the house by performing their duties for them at a mere half of their pay-rate.

As a rule, a gentleman attempts to be unobtrusive to the household's usual routines. He sleeps only when no one else is sleeping. He eats only whatever tidbits are thrown away or scraped into the garbage disposal. He washes his bed every morning, and he inspects the dirty clothes hamper for children or small animals every time someone places a piece of clothing in there.

Above all else, the gentleman arrives and leaves when he feels like it. As another person's guest, he understands that at all times he is to be treated as the most important individual in the house. Anything and everything he desires is at his fingertips.

# What to Do with Unwed Couples (Besides Laughing Behind Their Backs)

Throughout his lifetime, a gentleman might come to know many people who are scared to dedicate themselves to their sexual partners by getting married, especially if he is apt to hanging around with hippies, automobile plant workers, or other impoverished, low-class types of people. If the gentleman agrees with their lifestyle, he understands that he will be in no legal trouble if he decides to secretly sleep with one or both of the unmarried individuals. If he finds their unwed, yet cohabitating status to be repulsive, he does all that he can to make the couple split apart, which usually calls for him sleeping with one or both of the unmarried individuals.

If the couple is not ashamed to live together without first being married, the gentleman is not ashamed to discuss the couple's nontraditional relationship whenever he has the chance. For instance, a gentleman would not say, "Boy, you two make a cute couple." Instead, he would say, "I am so delighted that I know two people who are as irresponsible and indecisive as I am. Now if only someone would accept unlucky ol' me as their live-in lover so we could begin a quasi-committed relationship just like yours, I'd be temporarily satisfied."

If the couple is a gay or lesbian couple, the gentleman does not introduce them as such, assuming that any outsiders would be able to tell simply by taking a good look at the couple, who will either be wearing tacky, brightly-colored gay men's apparel or rugged, heavy-looking gay women's apparel.

If the couple does not want others to know of their co-existent relationship, they should inform people that the manner in which they live is none of their business and that marriage, like the churches in which they are held, are quickly fading and foolish institutions.

When corresponding with the unmarried couple, a gentleman should address the envelope to "My Two Good Friends Who Shun Matrimony." Letters to his gay and lesbian friends would be addressed to "Mr. Tad Follingsworth and Mrs. Enrique Gonzalez, the Hottest Gay Couple on the Planet" and "Mrs. Marge Flannigan and Mr. Greta von Sherpowski, Two Very Nice Lesbians."

# Handling Friends with Failed or Failing Marriages

When two of his married friends are having conflicts, a gentleman, being the impartial third party, fills the role of referee, listening to both friends and making judgments accordingly. Later, he strives to reconcile their differences by pulling both lovers aside and recalling funny or embarrassing moments with them.

If this fails to do the trick and the friends are madder than ever, the gentleman enlists the help of one of his other single friends, who happens to be cute, lonely, and a perfect match for him. Together, these two hatch a wild and unbelievable scheme that will somehow drive the two quarreling lovers into a series of ridiculous situations, and eventually, right back into each others' arms. Before it is all said and done, however, the gentleman and his co-conspirator friend (whom he was never attracted to before) will discover that they belong together, as well. An elegant and breathtaking wedding will then follow, the church pews packed with all of the weird and wacky characters who were encountered and subsequently paired off in the above hilarious and touching scheme. Roll credits.

If, despite the gentleman's noble actions, the couple permanently separates, the gentleman invites both divorced friends over and attempts to instigate another confrontation between the two in hopes that one or both of them will catch a glimpse of what they once had together. All of this should be done in the presence of other single friends, so the two divorcees do not feel awkward. Neither divorced person should know of the other's possible attendance, or else they might not show up and the night would be spoiled.

For example, a gentleman might tell Jeremy, who was once married to Regina, "Jeremy, old buddy, the tea party is going to be great. I'm inviting Arnold, Randall, Frank, Timothy, George, some girl, and Bobby."

If Jeremy asks who the girl is, the gentleman replies, "Just a girl you should meet. Don't worry. You'll like her."

Jeremy will then probably guess that the girl is Regina, since the gentleman has likely already done this sort of thing before. Jeremy, however, would be committing the social blunder here if he chooses to hang up on the gentleman and decline the tea party invitation. This should be the chief topic of discussion when the gentleman, Arnold, Randall, Frank, Timothy, George, Regina, and Bobby have their wonderful tea party.

If a gentleman says he will call, he calls to remind the person that he will be calling soon.

When parking his own car at a restaurant, a gentleman lets one of his passengers get out at the door to complain to management about the lack of valet parking. After that is settled, the gentleman and his friends find a new restaurant.

Since a gentleman assumes that his beliefs are all wrong and unimportant, he does not participate in discussions of politics or religion.

A gentleman realizes that senior citizens and mentally challenged people require a significant amount of special treatment from him. For instance, if a gentleman is purchasing a hot dog from an old, retarded street vendor and he realizes that the vendor probably does not add very much to society, he does not crudely push the man into the busy street behind him. Instead, he pushes the hot dog cart into the street, so that the vendor will chase it and get struck by a speeding vehicle, thereby ending his pitiful life and allowing a younger, less retarded person to enter into the wonderful industry of vending sausage-type meat products on the sidewalk.

When borrowing another person's property—whether it be a broken chain-saw, an exotic, yet tasteful brassiere, or a set of salad tongs with Looney Tune characters engraved on them—a gentleman keeps the borrowed items locked in a safe-deposit box at a local banking institution that he trusts. The objects should be securely kept there until he is ready to return them to their original owner.

A gentleman knows that a majority of his Christmas shopping can be done on the toy aisle of any grocery store.

If a male companion offers a gentleman a tasty nut, the gentleman refrains from giggling, opting instead to merely pinch the left testicle of he who offered the nut.

# 8

# A Gentleman on the job

A gentleman might prefer to carry work home from his office. He suspects that his co-workers are doing the same, so he attempts to bring more work home than anybody else.

A gentleman's business stationery is not for doodling. That's what the back of his hand and other people's business stationery is for.

If a gentleman is going to be more than one minute late for a business appointment, he calls in and says that he is dead.

When a gentleman resigns from his job, he never burns bridges. However, if his job was *burning* bridges, he should build a few bridges just to upset his old boss. Consequently, if his job was *building* bridges, he *should* burn bridges, but only if he plans on rebuilding those bridges out of recycled burnt bridge pieces. A gentleman forgets all of the above if his job had nothing to do with the construction or destruction of bridges.

# Gentleman vs. Answering Machine

A gentleman knows that in this modern world, identity theft runs rampant. Having an answering machine that divulges a lot of information about himself is like begging someone to steal his house and everything he's worked for throughout his life. Therefore, he reveals very little personal information when recording his answering machine's introductory message. Though he may be tempted to do so, he should not use his real name or phone number. He may actually prefer to include a few more false details to really fool those phone-wielding bandits.

Conversely, when leaving a message on other answering machines, the gentleman is just as distrusting and reluctant to disclose any pertinent information about himself. He may leave a message that contains an encoded version of his name, phone number, and reason for calling. He should mail the key for breaking the code to the person at least three days in advance of their calling.

If a gentleman receives a confusing or mysterious message, or if strange things begin happening in his life, he immediately destroys his answering machine and burns its remains in a rarely-used dumpster.

When someone asks a gentleman to take a message for one of his co-workers, he informs the person that he is not a secretary, though he will contact a secretary soon and have her take care of it. Of course, if the inquiring person is a secretary, he asks her to take the message down herself.

A gentleman knocks on any door he wishes to enter, whether it is open, closed, or broken in several pieces on the floor.

If a gentleman borrows a co-worker's pen, he purchases them two pens that are identical to the one he borrowed. That way, he may keep the borrowed one and not feel as guilty.

If a gentleman's office has large open spaces, he understands that his voice can easily be carried over long distances. Thus, when he has harsh words for a co-worker, he will not have to yell as loudly for the person to hear him clearly. The acoustics will allow him to conduct most of his business using just whispers, saving his voice for his home life.

# He Who Rules the Gentlemen

Though today's society is becoming increasingly liberal in its traditions, a gentleman remembers that all employees must completely submit to their employer. Even if he is employed by his own father, a gentleman should faithfully cater to his boss' every whim, no matter how outlandish, dangerous, or morally questionable the request.

A gentleman refers to every boss as "Boss," even if that boss is not necessarily his boss. A gentleman neither whines nor shows gratitude when his boss gives him a gift or takes something precious away from him. The boss knows what he or she has done and does not need the gentleman to call any more attention to the situation.

If a gentleman's boss invites him into his or her home, the gentleman treats their house as he would the office, keeping his desk area sterile and presentable, diligently foregoing all distractions in order to get some good work done, and engaging his boss in polite small talk whenever he passes him or her in the hallway.

A gentleman does not rely on a written résumé. He understands that nothing impresses an employer more than delivering a perfectly memorized oral résumé.

When the job interview ends, a gentleman sends a fruit basket, humorous postcard, and short thank-you letter to every one of the company's employees, a kind act which also serves to catch the eye of the gentleman's interviewer.

When being interviewed, a gentleman takes careful note of his would-be employer's clothing. This way, if the company hires him, he will be able to dress exactly like his boss, which all gentlemen know is a silent pledge of loyalty and gratitude.

At all times, a gentleman keeps a fresh umbrella in his bottom desk drawer, his car's trunk, his master bedroom, his garage, his left pants pocket, and in his personalized three-umbrella carrying case.

# Secrets of a Gentleman's Secretary

A gentleman rarely forgets that his secretary is a fellow human being. On such occasions when he does, the gentleman makes amends by presenting her with a coffee mug that has a cute, sarcastic message printed on it. If at any point in the future, the gentleman catches his secretary using a different mug than the one he gave her, he cuts her pay rate.

A gentleman makes his secretary feel more important by investing a lot of trust in her. For instance, she might be allowed to house and feed the gentleman's ailing grandmother, or he might put her in charge of videotaping and cataloguing his favorite television programs. In addition to completing all of her self esteem-boosting tasks, a gentleman expects his secretary to perform all of her normal operations, such as clipping the gentleman's toenails, finding the gentleman a plethora of suitable sex partners, and quickly reading whatever books the gentleman considers necessary for her to read.

At any time, a gentleman may choose to reward his secretary's exceptional performance by creating a handmade appreciation card out of construction paper, paint, glue, and macaroni. If he does not have the time or materials to craft such a card, he may have his secretary take care of it for him.

Even if they are not on speaking terms, a gentleman is sure to tell his secretary things like, "Little lady, I think you're tops," or "That Christmas sweater of yours really helps me get into the Christmas season." Offering such simple compliments can brighten the mood of an otherwise gloomy office environment, while simultaneously raising productivity levels by up to fifteen percent. A good secretary will type up a list of compliments every morning and post them for all of the office to see.

If a business trip calls for sharing a hotel room with his business associates, a gentleman knows that it is his responsibility to room with and protect all of the women with whom he is traveling. If the women refuse to let him carry out his gentlemanly duties, he sets up surveillance cameras to watch their room's entry points and posts himself as a permanent guard outside of their front door.

A gentleman updates his local phonebook on a regular basis.

A gentleman does not forward E-mails to people with whom he is angry. He knows that only his friends, not his enemies, deserve to read the thousands of hilarious or touching forwards that he receives in his virtual mailbox every morning.

Since he knows that an E-mail is essentially the same thing as a telephone call, a gentleman does not hesitate to ask his co-workers to either keep quiet or leave the room when he is sending or receiving E-mail.

A gentleman's business card is nobody's business but his own, and the same applies to the cards of others. When another businessperson offers his or her card to the gentleman, he politely places their card in his pocket and uses it for a bookmark or butter knife, if he can trust himself not to steal any peeks at it while doing so.

# E-mail E-tiquette

When using E-mail to correspond with another person, a gentleman sends a separate E-mail for each different subject he wishes to discuss, clearly indicating each subject in the specially-marked "Subject:" line. This helps the recipient keep their E-mail inbox tidy and categorized at all times. The gentleman may wish to include his full name, address, and phone number in the "From:" line. The "To:" line is where the gentleman lists the name of the primary person to whom the E-mail is being sent. The E-mail's "CC:" line, which stands for "Correspondent Cache" should always be filled with the gentleman's list of known E-mail addresses.

A gentleman understands that since E-mails are distributed across the incomprehensible void known as the World Wide Web, they are the least private methods of communication. Therefore, he is sure to convert every one of his E-mails into binary code, which can only be interpreted by the harmless computers who handle his messages, and not all of those meddlesome, perverted crooks who cruise cyberspace just to read other people's E-mails.

# What to Do in the Office Break Room

The office break room is the only place besides the restroom where a gentleman may do as he pleases. Once he crosses the barrier that divides the office area from the break room, the constraints of the office melt away and the gentleman knows that he is immediately among close friends, instead of co-workers, bosses, or secretaries. Here, the gentleman may eat, lounge, converse, or attempt to unravel the mysteries of human life, all the while remaining confident that he is not being watched, judged, or otherwise evaluated by his peers.

The break room's sink is a receptacle for liquids only, not the gentleman's dirty dishes. That's what the trash cans are for. A gentleman may sample, but not entirely consume, any leftovers that he finds in the communal refrigerator, as long as he does it while out of the sight of any co-workers passing by outside of the break room area.

A gentleman always brings ice cubes from his home to refill the ice trays at the office.

A gentleman comes up with a clever nickname for every receptionist with whom he has frequent dealings. This allows him to personalize any thank-you notes that he might send to them.

A gentleman fills the water cooler with freshly brewed coffee whenever he has the opportunity.

A gentleman offers a free, hands-on seminar to every employee whom he does not feel is adequately acquainted with the cleaning and operation of the office's coffeemaker.

A gentleman frequently writes or calls all of his business associates to determine whether they have changed their business address or phone number.

To encourage the social relationship between his business associates and himself, a gentleman insists upon using warmer, friendlier home phone numbers, instead of cold, detached business numbers.

If, in the midst of a large business meeting, a gentleman realizes that he will soil his trousers if he does not use the bathroom soon, he quickly composes a memo about it and passes it around the meeting. Once this is done, he stands and formally announces how long he expects his bathroom trip to last. If he does not live up to this estimation, he does not return to the meeting.

If a gentleman uses a sheet of paper in the copier machine, he immediately replaces it. This rule also applies to staplers, tape dispensers, and Post-It notes.

When on a business trip, a gentleman may abuse dangerous drugs and/or escort girls, but never his company's expense account.

A gentleman entertains his business clients as he would a child—by turning on the television and leaving the room.

At his work, a gentleman puts himself in a supervisory position whenever he can. By supervising his supervisors, he hopes to allow them more time to supervise him.

# 9

# A Gentleman's Equipment

Because he always has access to a soft, clean shirt, a gentleman can never run out of toilet paper.

A gentleman finds someone who will clean his house for him so that he may work enough extra hours to afford paying them to do so.

Before he settles on a dry cleaner, a gentleman subjects them to a rigorous questionnaire, which tests their knowledge of his starch preferences, current wardrobe constitution, and tuxedo rental history.

A gentleman always stores a professional-grade corkscrew in his back pocket.

# A Gentleman's List of Essential Items

Even though he may never use any of them, a gentleman should always have the following items:

- Half a dozen or more sturdy wooden toothpicks. (This way, he and at least five of his guests may safely enjoy the fine meats and cheeses of a delectable party platter.)

- Exactly half a dozen plastic toothpicks. (Some guests who also wish to enjoy the party platter's contents may be allergic to wood.)

- A few authentic wooden chopsticks. (In case of an extreme shortage of toothpicks or an exceptionally bountiful party platter, these may be whittled down into a number of fine makeshift toothpicks.)

- Exactly one dozen brittle wooden toothpicks. (After the party platter is consumed, some guests might like to clean their teeth of any uneaten morsels of cheddar or Italian sausage.)

Under his bathroom sink, the gentleman has:

- At least two varieties of cotton inserts that are used to soak up ovarian discharges. (Despite all of his efforts to predict this, a gentleman rarely knows when one of his female guests might begin her menstrual cycle.)

- At least two choices of adhesive strips of absorbent material that can be used as backup protection for a pair of panties. (Blood tends to spread outward from its source before clotting.)

- At least two forms of cleansing products that safely, refreshingly clean female genitalia. (When emptied by particularly unsanitary guests, these may be refilled with cooking oil.)

Every gentleman owns cloth blankets, as well as a few made of recycled news-papers.

The color of a gentleman's ink always matches the pen it comes from. That is why a gentleman never carries white, clear, or rainbow-colored pens.

At all times, a gentleman possesses a large, sturdy cardboard box in which he holds all of his other disassembled cardboard boxes. If he is prone to having an abundance of these cardboard boxes, a gentleman should have a larger, sturdier cardboard box in which to keep all of the cardboard boxes that hold his disassembled cardboard boxes.

A gentleman uses his personal stationery whenever he has to order more business stationery, because apparently he has run out of the appropriate type of stationery that he ordinarily uses to handle such business-related transactions.

# A Gentleman's List of Glassware

Because objects fashioned out of glass tend to break and become useless when dropped or thrown onto hard surfaces, a gentleman attempts to cushion all hard surfaces in his house. If it would be more practical to cover his glassware with a thick, spongy material, he does that instead.

On a gentleman's heavily-padded and sealed glassware shelf, there should be:

- At least nine old-fashioned Pizza Hut "E.T.: The Extraterrestrial" commemorative glasses, for eggnog, buttermilk, and other thick, fatty dairy drinks. (These are also handy when serving synthetic drinks like saline solution.)

- At least fourteen 44-oz. "Houston Rockets—1982 NBA Champions" plastic cups, perfect for serving cold drinks that exceed the volume of a standard 16-oz. glass. (These may also be used to serve warm or hot drinks that exceed 16-oz.)

- Roughly three multipurpose insulated "Garfield the Cat" mugs with removable lids and curlicue straws, the ideal receptacles for soups, small salads, alcoholic cocktails, white wines, or cake-like desserts. (For extra insulation, a gentleman may glue marshmallows around the mug's interior.)

- No more than seven "The South Will Rise Again" shot glasses, which may be used whenever the gentleman is entertaining a room full of ignorant Southern bigots.

A gentleman does not squander his hard-earned money on glasses for any beverages that may be consumed straight from their containers.

# A Gentleman's List of Chinaware

Even if he is homeless or an impoverished resident of a Third World country, a gentleman is able to present his guest with a basic dinner table. A gentleman's kitchen cabinets are always stocked with:

- At least five stunningly engraved sterling silver platters. (These may not be microwave-safe, but they can be used to transport other microwave-safe dishes from the refrigerator to the microwave.)

- Nearly ten authentic Native American clay dishes that compliment the silver platters. (If necessary, the gentleman may cover the dishes with a few coats of reflective silver paint.)

- Exactly five "banana boat" dishes of assorted colors, which may be used to serve banana splits. (If his guests are vegetarians and do not eat fruits, these dishes may also serve banana-less banana splits.)

- At least four child-size teacups and matching saucers.

- A set of personalized eating utensils that includes:

  - Four Teflon-coated spatulas

  - Four rubber-coated salad tongs

  - Four gold-trimmed butter scoops

  - Four titanium-encased pizza cutters

  - Four diamond-encrusted corncob holders

All of the gentleman's dishes and silverware should be rubbed down with a nice cloth and a high-quality brand of silver and china polishing cream before they are set on the table. Dinner guests will only eat off surfaces that are shiny enough to catch and hold their attention.

A gentleman owns instructional tapes for at least one spoken language, which should be English, unless the gentleman is fond of conversing with foreign people.

A gentleman hides his will and testament where no one would ever find it, so he and his loved ones might rest easy that his bequeathed possessions are safe and sound.

# A Gentleman and His Handkerchief

A gentleman's handkerchief is his most guarded and precious possession. He never offers it to others or uses it himself for fear of soiling it with bacteria-breeding phlegm or cloth-staining tears. He provides the handkerchief with a warm, cozy home in his breast pocket, where handkerchiefs prefer to rest during sunlight hours. He may feed the handkerchief tasty morsels from his meals as a treat.

After sundown, the gentleman carefully removes the handkerchief from his pocket, taking special care not to stir it from slumber. He then bathes it in lilac-scented buttermilk for an hour and dries it ever so lightly with a feather duster. Every night, the handkerchief sleeps in a hermetically-sealed, temperature-regulated chamber until the morning.

A gentleman does all of this without complaint and without ever being reminded to do it, for he realizes that the handkerchief will never betray him or leave his side until he is long dead, when it will then seek out the company of another living gentleman.

A gentleman keeps a good stock of premium cardboard pieces to write upon whenever he is hungry enough to make signs that ask for food donations.

# 10

# Hopelessly Difficult Etiquette: A Gentleman Takes on the Impossible

## Dealing with Royalty

A gentleman treats the meeting of royalty as any other casual occurrence. For instance, if a gentleman is being introduced to the queen of England, he offers her a pleasant smile and continues about his business. If it appears that she desires further physical contact or conversation with the gentleman, he stops whatever he is doing, politely curtsies, and addresses her with something like, "Mrs. Queen, I am incredibly sorry that my blood is nowhere near as noble as your own, for otherwise, we might become good acquaintances." If he hails from a different country than England, the gentleman then apologizes for trespassing upon her soil and returns to his home country.

Any time a country's ruler is in the room, he or she should be the only one wearing a hat. Out of courtesy, a gentleman removes his own hat and the hats of those who have not yet been properly trained in etiquette.

# Paying a Visit to the White House

A gentleman may never refuse an invitation to the White House, even if he inadvertently receives someone else's invitation. He understands that the White House was built by God, and he accepts that the mistaken invitation is just God's cunning way of sneaking him into the White House.

Once at the White House, the gentleman forgoes participating in any tours or silly diplomatic procedures. He is there to conduct social business with the president and the president only. Any presidential aides, secret service officers, or other White House personnel who stand in the gentleman's way should either be politely ignored or kindly asked to keep quiet.

Making tired jokes about the Clinton/Lewinsky scandal of years past is not allowed.

# Dealing with the President

A gentleman greets the president with a hearty handshake, knowing wink, and a firm pat on the back. As a matter of respect and consistency, a gentleman greets all politicians in such a manner, though he reserves the firm pat on the back for just the president.

Since the president has weightier matters on his mind, conversation should never stray from light and topical subjects, like favored brands of toothpaste, essential lawn care products, or short proposals concerning the extermination of all countries outside of America's borders.

If a woman should ever be elected president, the gentleman knows that the media loves a good presidential infidelity story, so he makes sure to converse only with her spouse, as long as she is married to a man.

A gentleman always remembers to keep his head at a higher level than the president's is.

# Kissing the Hands of Other People

A gentleman understands that all Europeans strictly follow the tradition of kissing the hand of a young lady for little to no reason. And if Europe's doing it, so should he.

If a lady extends her hand toward the gentleman, he quickly checks her palm and fingernails for any telltale signs of pollution. If her hand appears to be clean, he still scrubs it briskly with an antibacterial moist towelette before he will press his sterile lips to her skin.

If a piece of the lady's hand jewelry catches onto his facial hair, the gentleman does not panic, but instead sharply tugs the lady's hand away from his face, sacrificing the hair and flesh of his face for the expensive piece of jewelry.

# What to Do with the Pope

To acquire a meeting with the pope, a gentleman should be prepared to donate a small fortune to the Catholic Church. Financing the construction of a massive cathedral in any developing country will earn the gentleman a ticket and backstage pass for one of the pope's scheduled appearances.

For this rare and solemn occasion, a gentleman wears his holiest robe, which is the robe with the most gold trim and the greatest number of precious gems attached to it. The gentleman refers to the pope as "The Popish One" or "Thou Who Art Above All Men for Some Reason."

When the pope enters the room, everyone rushes to carry him over to his seat. The gentleman then falls in line with those who assist the pope in his various papal duties, which may require the gentleman to feed, burp, entertain, wipe, dress, or repeatedly lift the pope. He may also be responsible for propping the pope up for extended periods of time so that he appears to be awake and coherent. If, after this ordeal is finally over, the gentleman has not been formally introduced to or blessed by the pope, he does not complain and is content to wait until some other time.

# Entering the Realm of the Celebrity

Whenever a gentleman realizes that he is in the presence of a well-known sports figure, movie star, or some other grossly overvalued person, he does not make the celebrity uncomfortable by visibly acknowledging that he recognizes them. He does not ask them for an autograph or the opportunity to photograph them.

Instead, the gentleman figures out a more subtle, indirect method of obtaining the memento of his brush with supposed greatness. One successful strategy is for the gentleman to state that he is a world-famous photographer who is always looking for interesting models to shoot. He may then snap all the photographs he pleases, remembering to submit the pictures to every major publication in the world for quick cash.

Autographs are a bit trickier to obtain. Here, the gentleman should pose as a terminally ill child whose dying wish is to own a slip of paper that has been marked with the celebrity's signature.

After the gentleman gets all that he desires from the famous person, he creates a personal webpage that is devoted to the celebrity and auctions off the piece of celebrity memorabilia for a hefty sum of money that he will later "donate to charity."

# How to Address Various Other Important or Semi-Important People

• The Vice President of the United States of America
"Mr. (or Mrs.) Vice President of the United States of America"

• A Certified Clerk of Court
"Clerk Number _____"

• A Veteran of the Armed Forces
"Dear Faithful Bodyguard _____"

• A Televangelist
"Brother, But Only In Christ, Not In Blood, _____"

• The Reigning Prom Queen
"Her Royal Highness _____"

• A Foreign Dignitary
"Barbaric Leader of the Barbarians _____"

• A Burger King Employee
"Loyal Servant of the One True King _____"

• A Person Who Has a Royal-Sounding Last Name"
"Your Majesty _____"

# Difficult Dinner Table Scenarios

## Using a Finger Bowl

Some foods like lobster or watermelon require hard work and ingenuity in order to enjoy them. When a restaurant serves such foods, a finger bowl might be set upon the table for the dinner guests to clean their fingers of sticky or unpleasant juices.

The gentleman passes the finger bowl around the entire table before dipping his own fingers into it. Once this is done, he picks out any food particles, slices of fruit, or hairs that might be floating in the finger bowl.

He then carefully drinks the bowl's contents, replaces the objects that he previously picked out of the bowl, and signals for a waiter to take the finger bowl away.

## Eating Caviar

A gentleman delicately inspects each tiny fish egg for signs of embryonic life before he spreads it onto his cracker or bread crust. Eggs that appear to be fertilized may be incubated in a saucer of warm water or inside a hot, buttery dinner roll.

It will be a very difficult undertaking to find the eggs' biological mothers, but the gentleman should place any fertilized eggs well out of reach of the other party guests, who may unknowingly consume a precious life before it has a chance to begin. When the gentleman leaves the party, he does not return to his home until he has returned the eggs to theirs.

## Eating an Artichoke

Artichokes are tricky to eat because they are not necessarily meant for human consumption. A gentleman knows that each sharp-looking leaf that the artichoke points up at him is guarding a delicious, tender portion of the artichoke's heart. These valiant leaves do not discourage the gentleman and he presses on with knife and fork until he has sliced off all the leaves and drowned them in his dipping sauce.

Glorious, bleeding, and perhaps even still pumping, the artichoke's heart will then lie before the gentleman. He should devour this as quickly as possible to preserve the artichoke's precious life energy.

## Eating Snails

Some restaurants or parties might try to serve a gentleman something called escargot, or snails. The other party guests will be eating them, appearing to be having a wonderful time while doing so. But the gentleman knows better than to follow *those people* and consume snails.

Drawing as little attention to himself as possible, the gentleman swipes one of the emptied snail shells from one of the other guests' plates. He then uses the special tongs and miniature fork to pretend that he is enjoying the snail meat just like everybody else.

No one is any wiser of his abstinence and he doesn't have to poison his body with snail meat.

## Eating the Sorbet Scoop

While attending some banquets or formal dinners, a small scoop of lightly-sweetened sorbet is brought out after the main course. Though he may consider this to be hardly a fulfilling dessert, the gentleman gratefully eats his sorbet. And since he knows that dessert comes at the conclusion of every meal, the gentleman refuses to eat anything further.

# The End of the Guide: A Gentleman's Final Words

A gentleman knows that his sole purpose in life is to selflessly facilitate the lives of others in every conceivable way. He never forgets that whatever dreams, desires, or loves that he may have are inconsequential in the grand scheme of the universe.

If the fate of the world did not depend so greatly upon the gentleman's unwavering assistance, then the gentleman would have been born as some other type of person, and not as a gentleman. This confusing, incongruous belief about a gentleman's control and submission to a predestined fate is the philosophical cornerstone of gentlemanism.

The highest honor for a gentleman is acquiring the title of True Perfect Gentleman.

There is no such thing as a True Perfect Gentleman.

Thus, every True Perfect Gentleman calmly understands that he simply does not exist. Everyone in the world is content with this, for if you were to ever come across a True Perfect Gentleman—someone who could warp their will and lifestyle in accordance to such a ridiculous point of "refined" behavior—he would be such a little bitch.

But if it were possible for such a man, nay, a gentleman, and I'm talking a Gentleman with a capital G, to walk this earth, that man would be me, Sir Gentleman Brock LaBorde, Esquire, for I am as close to perfection as can be. And none of you would-be gentlemen readers shall attain the God-like gentlemanistic level that I have, for I am withholding one tiny rule from you all.

Yes, this brilliant, comprehensive guide is an unfinished work.

For if you knew this one last thing, this miniscule, barely-used, insane behavioral restriction, then you would be my etiquette equal…and I just can't have that.

I think that I shall go to the grave with this secret, likely by the depraved, filthy hands of one of you, I imagine.

Until then, good luck with your manners and please stop sending me requests to bless or heal your stupid children.

Thank you.

You're welcome.

*You may stop reading this book now. Thank you.*

0-595-34152-7